Wigan Athletic F. C., An A–Z

Wigan Athletic F. C., An A–Z

by Dean Hayes

Palatine Books, 1995

Wigan Athletic F. C., An A–Z
by Dean Hayes

Published in 1995 by Palatine Books,
an imprint of Carnegie Publishing Ltd, 18 Maynard Street, Preston

Text copyright © Dean Hayes, 1995

Typeset in Monotype Ehrhardt by Carnegie Publishing, Preston
Printed in the UK by Redwood Books

British Library Cataloguing-in-Publication Data
A catalogue record for this book is available from the British Library
ISBN 1–874181–16–0

Contents

Author's Preface

Dean Hayes is a Lancashire man through and through. This is his sixth book in an A–Z look at Lancashire's football clubs and follows Blackburn Rovers, Oldham Athletic, Bolton Wanderers, Everton and Manchester City, all of which have been highly successful.

A former Primary School Headteacher and a member of the prestigious 92 club, he is now a freelance writer.

This book is dedicated to Latics supporters everywhere, but particularly to my many friends (and that includes umpires!) in the Wigan and District Cricket League.

Acknowledgements

Every reader will agree that the quality of photographs greatly enhances the appeal of this book so I am extremely grateful to Wigan Athletic Football Club and *the Wigan Observer* for the use of their pictures.

However, should photographs from an outside source have been inadvertently reproduced, following previous use in the club's programmes, without acknowledgement, please accept the author's apologies and let him know so that this omission may be rectified in any subsequent impression.

Thanks to individuals are due to Colin Walls, Steven Lunt, Jim Gaskell, Gordon Allen, Bernard Eccles and Jim McEwan.

Abandoned Matches

An abandoned match may be defined as one that is called off by the referee, *whilst it is in progress*, because the conditions do not permit it to be completed.

Generally speaking, far fewer matches are abandoned in modern times because, if there is some doubt about the ability to play the full game, the match is more likely to be postponed. However, the match against Bolton Wanderers at Burnden Park on 28 February 1989 was abandoned at half-time with the score at 0–0. The reason given was that the pitch was waterlogged, but most fans at the game (both Latics and Wanderers) thought the pitch was no worse than when the game kicked off!

There have been some unusual reasons why Latics games have been abandoned. In Latics' first season, they were beating Congleton Town 7–0 shortly after half-time, when on a bitterly cold day, the match was abandoned with Congleton being reduced to six men, the others having been taken off suffering from exposure. Nevertheless, Latics won the re-arranged fixture 6–2.

In the 1935–36 crunch game with Altrincham, the referee stopped play after 76 minutes following a crowd invasion after he had turned down two penalty appeals.

Season	Competition	Opponents	Venue	Score
1932–33	Cheshire League	Congleton Town	Home	7–0
1935–36	Cheshire League	Altrincham	Home	0–1
1935–36	Cheshire League	Stalybridge Celtic	Away	6–1
1936–37	Cheshire League	Hurst	Home	8–2
1936–37	Cheshire League	Stalybridge Celtic	Away	1–0
1938–39	Cheshire League	Manchester N.E.	Away	1–2
1945–46*	Cheshire League	Stalybridge Celtic	Away	5–2

Season	Competition	Opponents	Venue	Score
1948–49	Lancs Combination Cup	Horwich R.M.I.	Home	5–0
1955–56	Lancs Junior Cup	Horwich R.M.I.	Home	1–1
1956–57	Lancashire Combination	Bacup Borough	Away	1–2
1959–60	Lancashire Combination	Skelmersdale United	Away	2–0
1960–61	Lancs Combination Cup	Chorley	Home	1–1
1960–61	Liverpool N-L Snr Cup	South Liverpool	Away	1–2
1962–63	Cheshire League	Winsford United	Home	1–2
1964–65	Liverpool N-L Snr Cup	Prescot Cables	Away	2–3
1968–69	Northern Premier League	Gateshead	Away	0–0
1968–69	Lancs Junior Cup	Great Harwood	Home	0–0
1969–70	Lancs Floodlit Cup	Skelmersdale United	Home	2–0
1979–80	F.A. Cup	Northwich Victoria	Away	3–0
1986–87	F.L. Division 3	Bournemouth	Home	1–1
1988–89	F.L. Division 3	Bolton Wanderers	Away	0—0

* The scoreline stood and the match was not replayed.

Age

Youngest

The youngest player to appear in a Football League fixture for Wigan Athletic F.C. is Steve Nugent, who played in our match at Leyton

Orient (0–1) on 16 September 1989, when he was 16 years and 132 days old.

Oldest

The oldest player to line up in a Latics' first team in the Football League is Roy Tunks. Roy was approaching his 37th birthday when he last turned out for Wigan, at Blackpool (0–0) on 24 October 1987. In fact, Tunks had a remarkably long career, having made his Football League début for Rotherham United when he was only 16 years of age.

Roy Tunks—the oldest player to line up in a Latics side in the Football League.

Aldershot

In March 1992 the liquidator called in to supervise the winding up of the 'Shots' confirming to the Football League that no offers had been received for the Fourth Division club. Latics first met Aldershot in the club's first League season. In fact, that first season saw Aldershot come to Wigan with a run of sixteen games without defeat, but in an entertaining game, goals from Moore and Houghton (2) saw Latics win 3–2, though Aldershot gained revenge with the only goal of the game at the Recreation Ground.

The next two seasons saw Wigan complete the double over Aldershot—2–1 (h) and 3–0 (a) in 1979–80 and 1–0 (h) and 1–0 (a) in

 Paul Jewell claims the first of his hat-trick goals.

1980–81. The following season saw the clubs meet on four occasions. The honours were shared in the League with each side winning at home, but in the League Cup, Latics won 3–2 on aggregate.

It was 1987–88 before the two sides met again, and though the 'Shots' won 3–2 at home, they lost 0–4 at Springfield Park. The game was featured on 'Football Focus' as Latics were going for promotion at the time. Paul Jewell hit a hat-trick and missed a penalty that night! The following season was the last occasion the two sides met. Aldershot triumphed 3–1 at home, but the Latics won at Springfield Park 2–1, with goals from Thompson and Griffiths.

Aldershot never won at Springfield Park and of course now due to their folding never will!

Amateur International Match

Springfield Park staged an Amateur International match between England and Scotland on Friday 24 March 1972. England won the game 4–0 in front of 2,704 spectators.

Appearances

The players with the highest number of Football League appearances for Wigan Athletic F.C. are as follows:

Kevin Langley	1981–1994	317
Colin Methven	1979–1986	296
Alex Cribley	1980–1987	271
Roy Tunks	1981–1987	245
John Butler	1982–1988	245
Allen Tankard	1988–1993	205
Peter Houghton	1978–1983	195
David Lowe	1982–1987	188
Bryan Griffiths	1988–1993	187
Graham Barrow	1981–1986	179

Consecutive Football League Appearances

Three players have made over one hundred consecutive appearances immediately following their league débuts for the club:

Tommy Gore, 102: début 19 August 1978 v. Hereford United (a) 0–0
Jeff Wright, 110: début 19 August 1978 v. Hereford United, (a) 0–0
Colin Methven, 134: début 13 October 1979 v. Doncaster Rovers (a) 1–3

Non-League Appearances

The following players headed the number of appearances made in the other league competitions that Latics have played in:

Cheshire League:	Derek Houghton	259
Lancashire Combination:	Harry Parkinson	342
Northern Premier League	Ian Gillibrand	412

During the 1950–51 season, Harry Parkinson finally missed a game after 210 consecutive appearances (includes 1 abandoned match). In

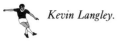
Kevin Langley.

1967–68, Derek Houghton who had played over 500 games in a ten-season career was swopped for Norman Sykes.

Attendances at Springfield Park

Opponents	Date	Competition	Attendance
Individual matches: highest in the Football League			
Bolton Wanderers	26 December 1983	Division 3	10,045

Opponents	Date	Competition	Attendance
Plymouth Argyle	19 April 1986	Division 3	9,485
Barnsley	3 March 1979	Division 4	9,427
Grimsby Town	23 August 1978	Division 4	9,227
Bournemouth	4 May 1982	Division 4	9,021
Bolton Wanderers	26 December 1984	Division 3	8,871
Mansfield Town	8 May 1982	Division 4	8,517
Port Vale	13 April 1979	Division 4	8,452
Portsmouth	3 February 1979	Division 4	8,289
Hartlepool United	16 April 1979	Division 4	8,217

Lowest

There have been quite a number of League matches at Springfield Park in recent seasons in which attendances have been under 2,000. The lowest last season was 1,231 against Chesterfield on 30 August 1994.

Other games at Springfield Park

Opponents	Date	Competition	Attendance
Hereford United	1953–54	F.A. Cup Round 2	27,526
Newcastle United	1953–54	F.A. Cup Round 3	26,500
Millwall	1934–35	F.A. Cup Round 3	25,304
Torquay United	1934–35	F.A. Cup Round 2	20,003
Peterborough United	1970–71	F.A. Cup Round 2	17,180
Mansfield Town	1974–75	F.A. Cup Round 2	15,560
Aston Villa	1981–82	F.L. Cup Round 4	15,362
Sheffield Wednesday	1977–78	F.A. Cup Round 2	13,871
Scarborough	1953–54	F.A. Cup Round 1	12,692
Leeds United	1986–87	F.A. Cup Round 6	12,250

Latics' biggest ever home League gate is 11,827 in our first ever season on Saturday 22 October 1932 against Cheshire League leaders, Northwich Victoria—Latics won the match by the incredible margin of 9–0.

The largest ever crowd at Springfield Park was the 30,611 when Wigan Borough entertained Sheffield Wednesday in the F.A. Cup of 1928–29.

Wigan Athletic's average home attendances since our admission to the Football League have been as follows:

1978–79	6,701	1987–88	3,759
1979–80	5,896	1988–89	3,151
1980–81	4,411	1989–90	2,758
1981–82	5,839	1990–91	2,889
1982–83	4,437	1991–92	2,862
1983–84	3,898	1992–93	2,598
1984–85	3,265	1993–94	1,897
1985–86	4,353	1994–95	1,872
1986–87	3,397		

Away

Season	Opponents	Competition	Score
		Best away wins	
1948–49	Rossendale United	Lancashire Combination	6–3
1954–55	Nelson	Lancashire Combination	9–4
1964–65	Darwen	Cheshire League	7–0
1965–66	Stafford Rangers	Cheshire League	6–1
1975–76	Great Harwood	Northern Premier League	7–3

Season	Opponents	Competition	Score
1977–78	Lancaster City	Northern Premier League	6–1
1981–82	Scunthorpe United	F.L. Division 4	7–2
1990–91	Swansea City	F.L. Division 3	6–1

Worst Away Defeats

1937–38	Stockport County Res.	Cheshire League	1–8
1937–38	Witton Albion	Cheshire League	1–6
1945–46	Hyde United	Cheshire League	0–8
1945–46	Witton Albion	Cheshire League	0–7
1946–47	Chester Res.	Cheshire League	4–9
1946–47	Runcorn	Cheshire League	3–8

Highest scoring away draws

1934–35	Macclesfield Town	Cheshire League	4–4
1952–53	Horwich R.M.I.	Lancashire Combination	4–4
1955–56	New Brighton	Lancashire Combination	4–4
1960–61	Bacup Borough	Lancashire Combination	4–4
1980–81	Scunthorpe United	F.L. Division 4	4–4
1987–88	Notts County	F.L. Division 3	4–4

Most Away Wins in a Season   16 in 1953–54 (Lancashire Combination)

Fewest Away Wins in a Season   1 in 1945–46 (Cheshire League) and 1958–59 (Lancashire Combination)

Most Away Defeats in a Season   16 in 1945–46 (Cheshire League) and 1958–59 (Lancashire Combination)

Fewest Away Defeats in a Season	1 in 1970–71 (Northern Premier League)
Most Away Goals in a Season	54 in 1965–66 (Cheshire League)
Fewest Away Goals in a Season	15 in 1958–59 (Lancashire Combination)

Kenny Banks

One of the Latics' greatest ever servants, Kenny Banks has been player, trainer, coach, physiotherapist, temporary manager, the lot!

There were times in Kenny's playing career when big clubs were keen to sign him. Like many a Latics player, he represented the town whilst a schoolboy, but it was not until he left school that League clubs started to notice the stocky youngster who could kick well with either foot. Bolton and Southport were in a race to sign him and it was Southport who got his signature. In those days, it was normal for youngsters to play as amateurs in the League until their clubs had assessed them properly. He so impressed the fans in pre-season games prior to the 1947–48 season, that he was signed professional, much to the annoyance of Aston Villa who were keen to sign him.

Insisting on keeping up his job outside football, he only played as a part-time professional for the Haig Avenue side. After three years with Southport, he was placed on the transfer list at £1,000 and various clubs were interested, but they wanted him as a full-timer.

Kenny Banks' allegiance had always been to Wigan, so when the manager of Athletic at that time, Ted Goodier, found him a position at a local factory, he was more than happy to sign for the club.

In his years at Springfield Park, Kenny enjoyed his best moments in football. The Latics won the Lancashire Combination three years running, went up to St James's Park and drew with the mighty Newcastle United 2–2 and all in all proved that they were one of the best non-league sides in the history of the game.

After his playing career was over, he stayed with the Latics and when election to the Football League came along, it was, for Kenny Banks, a fitting reward for the many years' service he had given to Wigan Athletic at every level.

Barclays Performance of the Week

It was Latics' 6–1 win in the Third Division match at Swansea City on 6 April 1991 that caught the eye of England manager Graham Taylor and his fellow selectors and thus brought us this prestigious award for the first time.

Three weeks later in the home game against Cambridge United, a local boys club from Shevington received a new set of strip and a cheque for £300, while the Wigan directors received a silver trophy as a memento of the award.

Graham Barrow

In his playing days with the Latics, Graham Barrow helped the club to promotion to Division Three in 1981–82 and scored 36 goals in 179 League appearances before moving to Chester City in 1986, where he played in over 200 games for the Blues.

A long-time friend of Harry McNally, Barrow played under him at Altrincham, Wigan and Chester and joined the former Latics' boss at Chester for a tribunal-fixed fee of £6,000. Employed as player-coach, he became assistant manager in 1988 and took over from McNally after a poor start to the 1992–93 season.

However, things did not improve much after he took over and at the end of their first season in the new Deva Stadium, Chester were relegated. Finishing runners-up to Shrewsbury Town in 1993–94, Chester were immediately promoted.

Barrow's Springfield Park arrival a year or so ago sparked a dramatic improvement in fortunes. The Latics' revival under Barrow was so emphatic that there was a period when the air was thick with talk of a possible play-off place. After starting the 1995–96 season with a squad

containing a good balance of eager youth and mature experience, Graham Barrow was rather surprisingly sacked in October 1995

Bolton Wanderers

The clubs first met at Springfield Park on Boxing Day 1983. The morning kick-off proved a hit, with a crowd of 10,045, Wigan's best league gate, seeing a Jeff Chandler goal win the game for Bolton. Earlier, Wanderers' 'keeper Simon Farnworth pulled off a penalty save from Bolton old boy Steve Taylor.

Wigan made their first visit to Burnden Park in April 1984 and took maximum points thanks to a 13th minute goal by Steve Johnson. In 1984–85, a Gerry McElhinney own-goal gave Latics the points at Springfield Park, whilst a Jeff Chandler penalty did likewise for Bolton at Burnden Park. Victories by a single goal litter the record between the two clubs, but more goals came the following term when Wigan won 2–1 at Burnden on New Years Day. This game saw Bolton's Steve Thompson sent off. However, this was not as straight forward as it seems as the referee, Ken Walmsley, has since admitted that when he sent Thompson off, he thought he had already booked the Bolton number 8, but it was in fact the Wigan number 8 (Graham Barrow) who had been previously booked! In the return match the following March, Bolton ended the Latics' record league run of 33 home games without defeat, winning 3–1 at Springfield Park.

In 1986–87, the Latics completed the double, with a 2–1 scoreline resulting in their favour in each case.

Though they didn't meet in the League the following season, the Latics beat their neighbours 5–4 on aggregate in the League Cup. Bolton had won 3–2 at Springfield Park, but a Bobby Campbell hat-trick gave Latics a 3–1 victory away from home to secure the tie.

Back in the League the following season, the first game at Burnden Park was abandoned at half-time due to a waterlogged pitch with the match goalless. When the match was played again, the sides fought out the first league draw between the clubs, with former Wanderer Wayne Entwistle netting for Latics. The return match at Springfield Park also ended 1–1. The following season saw Latics storm into a two goal lead

Steve Johnson, who scored the Latics' goal on the visit to Burnden Park in April 1984.

inside the first five minutes thanks to a Scott McGarvey free-kick and a Mark Hilditch chip, only for Bolton to win 3–2. At Springfield Park, a goal from Bryan Griffiths and an own goal by Bolton captain Phil Brown, gave Wigan victory.

In 1990–91 an error by Phil Hughes in the Latics goal allowed Julian Darby to score a second goal for the Wanderers and though Bryan Griffiths pulled one back from the penalty spot, the home side held out. The result was reversed at Springfield Park with Patterson and Griffiths (penalty) getting the Latics' goals.

Wayne Entwistle, who played for both Wigan and Bolton.

In 1991–92 Latics' old boy Tony Kelly scored an own goal to give Wigan a share of the spoils at Burnden Park, whilst a Gary Worthington goal at Springfield Park also produced a 1–1 draw.

In 1992–93, Latics lost 1–2 at Burnden Park in spite of going ahead through a Gary Powell goal and were beaten 0–2 at home in front of their biggest crowd of the season, 5,408.

Our overall record in the League against Bolton Wanderers is as follows:

P	W	D	L	F	A
18	7	4	7	21	22

Allan Brown

Allan Brown was appointed player-manager of Wigan Athletic in 1964 and thus began the formation of one of the most attractive teams in many years. Despite the fact that it was his first managerial job, he soon got into the swing of things. He began signing players immediately—Les Campbell, Ralph Gubbins, Bert Llewellyn, John Ryan and Roy Wilkinson—men who proved to be great favourites with the fans.

The Latics' team, superbly drilled and organised by Brown, won the Cheshire League under his guidance and no one will forget the part Brown, the player, had in the set-up. Cool, thoughtful and a physical fitness fanatic, he made a tremendous impact at Springfield Park.

Brown's success with Wigan Athletic soon had the League clubs after his signature and just 18 months after joining the Latics he left to join Luton Town, one of his former clubs.

He managed Torquay United and Blackpool, but there were many qualities Allan Brown brought to the game as a player-manager that seemed to elude him when he hung up his boots and concentrated solely on management.

Bull's Head

The Bull's Head Public House in Wigan town centre was the meeting place of a group of prominent men who gathered together with the idea of forming another 'senior' soccer team for Wigan. The men, seven of them, together formed a steering committee with the purpose of getting a new club off the ground.

President of the committee was Joseph Howarth, destined to be the club's first chairman and he was backed up in his unstinting efforts by Jack Farrimond, who was appointed secretary, Charles Ostick, George Woods, Peter Dwyer, Tom Heywood and Richard Farrimond, Jack's father. One other man was in on the formation, the club's first manager, Charlie Spencer.

The idea for a new club was mooted, it is believed, in the Pagefield Hotel, when two of the gentlemen decided to do something about there being no senior football team in the town.

An advert was placed in the *Wigan Observer* inviting all interested parties to attend a meeting at the Queen's Hall. There was some doubt about the numbers who would attend but no one needed to have worried—the Queen's Hall was packed!

Café Royal

London's Café Royal was the location of Wigan Athletic's election to the Football League on Friday 2 June 1978.

After tying with Southport 26 votes each—a re-vote resulted in Wigan being elected by 29 votes to 20, and after 34 disappointments, Wigan were in. The Wigan representatives at the meeting, namely Arthur Horrocks, Jack Farrimond and Ian McNeill, immediately returned to Springfield Park to be greeted by numerous jubilant supporters.

Captains

When Latics won the Cheshire League Championship in 1933–34 for what was the first of three consecutive seasons, it was George O'Dell who skippered the side.

John Higgins went straight from the captaincy of the then Division One side Bolton Wanderers to the captaincy of the Latics on joining us in 1961.

It was Ian Gillibrand who stepped onto Hereford United's Edgar Street pitch at 2.50 p.m. on Saturday 19 August 1978 to make history, and who could blame the popular Latics skipper as he shed a tear.

Colin Methven was the Latics captain when they lifted the Freight Rover Trophy at Wembley on Saturday 1 June 1985 after defeating Brentford by 3 goals to 1.

Central League

The Central League was formed in 1912 by the Northern and Midland giants of the Football League as specifically a reserve team league. The first ever winners were not, however, giants, but Lincoln City—who won it with 48 points out of a possible 64 and then immediately withdrew from the League, never to return.

The League continued even during the First World War when its regionalised nature enabled it to carry on whilst the Football League was forced into abeyance.

From its early days, the League was a difficult one to win, but from 1968–69, Liverpool reserves lifted the title for eleven of the next thirteen seasons. But as the men from Anfield strengthened their grip on the League, the standard of football started to drop. Something had to be done to revitalise the League and in the time of recession, to enable clubs to field two teams whilst cutting playing staff.

The solution came in two forms—the League was expanded from 22 in one division to 32 in two. The fixtures were changed from Saturday to mid-week, thus enabling managers not only to utilise their dwindling numbers of players more effectively, but also to watch the games themselves. And so, in June 1982, Wigan Athletic got its chance, along with twelve others, to apply for one of the ten new places in the League. After so many unsuccessful applications to join the Football League, the Latics' representatives would not have been surprised to have failed at their first attempt—but, as luck would have it, they polled 18 votes and were elected. Their first game was at home to Burnley, Latics winning by 3–0. This was followed by a 0–0 draw at Chesterfield . . . Latics losing their first home match 0–2 to Bradford City in their fourth game. At the end of the 1983–84 season, Latics had to apply for re-election, but the next season saw the young Latics side, who combined hard work, enthusiasm and talent, gain promotion to the First Division.

The Latics v. Preston North End reserves match saw father playing against son. Ex-Manchester United and Northern Ireland international Sammy McIllroy played against Sammy McIllroy junior who played for Latics. Also at reserve team level, the game against Oldham Athletic at Boundary Park was abandoned after 54 minutes due to

floodlight failure. Wigan were winning 3–2 at the time and around ten minutes after the lights failed they finally gave up—Oldham winning the re-match!

Centuries

Goals

The Latics have scored a century of goals in a non-League season on twelve occasions. Our highest tally of 153 goals from 42 matches was achieved in 1934–35 when we won the Cheshire League Championship for the second time. It was also the season when we scored 106 League goals at Springfield Park.

In the Football League, our highest number of goals in a season came in 1986–87 when we scored 83, with Bobby Campbell and David Lowe both scoring 16.

There are eight instances of individual players who have scored 100 or more goals for the Latics. Harry Lyon is our greatest goalscorer with 273 strikes in his Wigan career (1962–1969) while Billy Lomax scored 189 goals between 1949 and 1955. Other centurions are Bert Llewellyn (147), Horace Thomas (132), John Rogers (125), Jackie Lyon (122), Micky Worswick (112) and George Scott (102).

Appearances following début

Three Latics players have made over a hundred consecutive appearances immediately after making their Football League début. Tommy Gore (102) and Jeff Wright (110) made their Football League débuts for Latics in our opening game of the 1978–79 season, while Colin Methven (134) is the most recent Latics man to reach this target.

In 1950–51 Harry Parkinson finally missed a game after 210 consecutive appearances (including 1 abandoned match).

Certainties!

After the magnificent season of 1970–71, optimism was high that surely the Football Association could not possibly refuse the Latics League status. The mood of optimism was captured perfectly by the *Wigan Observer*.

'Unless soccer has gone insane, I will challenge all-comers to argue that Wigan are not now a certainty to be in the Football League by the end of May.'

The Football League meeting was held at the Café Royal. Lincoln City, Barrow, Hartlepool and Newport County all applied for re-election. All got it with 47, 38, 33 and 33 votes respectively. Hereford came next with 22, whilst Wigan polled the terribly disappointing total of 14.

In Wigan the news was seen as an insult to both the club and the town as a whole. There had to be a scapegoat and Ken Cowap, the club chairman had the blame laid firmly at his feet. Prior to the meeting, Mr Cowap had distributed a gift of a £2 Parker pen to each voting representative. It seemed as if that small gesture of goodwill and publicity rebounded and was construed as an attempt to unfairly influence the voting. Whether or not it did affect the voting was debatable—yet the club picked up 4 fewer votes than the previous season, though they had achieved such fantastic results.

The following year when Hereford United were admitted to the League, they made everyone a present of a china bull, and it did not affect their vote tally!

Chelsea

The Latics were paired with Chelsea in Cup competitions in the 1980s on three occasions.

The first of these was on 14 January 1980 when future Chelsea manager Ian McNeill was in charge of the Latics. Chelsea were top of the Second Division having beaten Newcastle United 4–0 a few days

earlier. This F.A. Cup Third Round clash at Stamford Bridge was settled after 40 minutes when diminutive midfield terrier Tommy Gore whipped the ball off the foot of colleague Jeff Wright before floating it gently over Peter Borota and into the net for the only goal of the game.

Chance of revenge for Chelsea came quickly. Two seasons later, the teams came out of the bag together, this time in the Third Round of the Football League Cup. And again, Latics scored a notable victory, this time at Springfield Park. John Bumstead gave Chelsea a 12th minute lead, but then Latics hit back with three goals in an incredible period of ten minutes. Mark Wignall scored from 25 yards. Clive Evans flicked in Kevin Shelton's cross before Wignall cracked the most spectacular shot of the night from ten yards outside the penalty area to made it 3–1. Before the interval Mike Fillery reduced the deficit, but Les Bradd's first goal for Wigan in the 53rd minute settled matters irretrievably. The now Chelsea chairman, Ken Bates, was at the time vice-chairman of the Latics.

 Paul Jewell scores for Latics in the 2–2 draw at Chelsea.

The sides met again in the F.A. Cup Third Round at Stamford Bridge in the 1984–85 season when goals from Paul Jewell and Mick Newell gave Latics a 2–2 draw and brought the Pensioners back to Springfield Park for a replay.

Unfortunately, there was no fairy-tale ending, with Chelsea winning 5–0 and Kerry Dixon scoring four of the goals. It was Latics' first home defeat in the F.A. Cup since the referee blew for time with Alf Craig's shot on its way into the Tranmere net in the 1–0 defeat on 28 November 1966.

Cheshire League

Wigan Athletic were elected to the Cheshire League at the expense of Manchester Central. The first game took place on 27 August 1932, as the Latics went down 2–0 at the hands of Port Vale reserves in front of 5,106 spectators who paid a total of £161 to watch the game.

The team playing in red and white shirts with black shorts and socks finished a creditable fifth in their first season, before surpassing all expectations by winning the League Championship in three consecutive seasons thereafter.

It was during the 1935–36 season (when this excellent team also won the Lancashire Junior Cup) that centre-forward Jack Roberts set a club record of 64 goals—a record that stood for 29 years.

When football resumed after the war, the Cheshire League committee in their wisdom imposed a post-war restriction on the wages of £2 per week. Many of the club's pre-war players were by this time either too old for the game or for some reason unavailable. The result of these circumstances was that the Latics finished bottom of the League.

The Cheshire League then passed a decision that shocked the town of Wigan. In a sensational meeting, Athletic's application for re-election was defeated, and so a club that had virtually been invincible pre-war found itself ejected—to make way for Winsford United.

The town and the club's pride was salvaged, for along with Accrington Stanley, the club was elected to the Lancashire Combination.

By 1960–61, the management of the club felt the team should be competing with much stronger opposition, so a decision was taken to apply to join the Cheshire League.

Wigan Athletic won the Cheshire League for the first time in 1933–34. Here they are with the Championship Trophy. The manager Charlie Spencer is fourth from the right on the back row.

In 1964–65 the side chalked up honours as though they were going out of fashion. As well as lifting the Cheshire League Championship, the side won the Cheshire League Cup and the Liverpool Non-League Senior Cup. The team went through an unbeaten run of 29 games between 5 December 1964 and Easter Monday 1965, whilst Harry Lyon, with 66 goals, smashed Jack Roberts' record.

The club's final season in the Cheshire League was 1967–68 for the following season, the Latics competed in the opening season of the Northern Premier League.

The club's full record in the Cheshire League is as follows:

P	W	D	L	F	A	Pts
668	361	111	196	1634	1063	833

Chorley

Wigan Athletic v. Chorley was a fixture that always seemed to command special attention, for it always provided a good example of all that is best about non-League football—the intense rivalry between both fans and players, the 'local derby' atmosphere and the extra effort that goes into every tackle.

Over the years Chorley always seemed to be one of the teams that were able to give us a hard game, win, lose or draw, and on many occasions succeeded in very important games.

The meetings between the two clubs invariably proved to be one of the highspots of the season for both sides with many outstanding memories. One that older supporters may recollect was at Chorley on 14 April 1951 when Latics ran out winners 7–1 in a Lancashire Combination match. The goalscorers were Bootle 2, Pollard 2, Owen 2 and Lomax.

Or do you remember for instance the two great goals scored by John Fielding and Alan Herron which gave Latics a Junior Cup win in 1959–60? And that Trevor Hitchen-inspired F.A. Cup success before Wigan beat Southport in the First Round proper? Or again, a Wigan goalkeeper named Smith who broke a finger in a match at Victory Park when Latics also had a Malaysian inside-forward Lenny Leishing in their line-up?

Latics' full record v. Chorley:

P	W	D	L	F	A
65	33	12	20	122	104

Clean Sheet

This is the colloquial expression to describe a goalkeeper's performance when he does not concede a goal.

Only three Latics goalkeepers have ever had 20 or more clean sheets in a season: Dennis Reeves had 22 in 1972–73; Peter Eales had 21 in 1975–76 and Harold Woolley had 20 in 1947–48.

At Football League level, both John Brown (1978–79) and Roy Tunks (1983–84) kept 17 clean sheets from 42 appearances.

Colours

The first ever team to represent Wigan Athletic played in red and white shirts, with black shorts and socks.

When Latics visited Runcorn for the opening fixture of the 1946–47 Cheshire League season, it was the first time that the club wore blue and white. The strip was adopted mainly because the sports shop who supplied the kit could only supply the blue strip!

When Latics took to playing in blue and white stripes in season 1977–78, the man responsible for donating the playing gear was a certain Peter Swales, former chairman of Manchester City. The first home match in the strip was against Goole Town on Saturday 27 August 1977 in a game Latics won 2–0 with two John Wilkie goals.

After a number of seasons wearing all blue shirts and shorts with a red and white trim and blue stockings, the club changed at the beginning of the 1993–94 season to blue and black stripes. The club changed colours again at the outset of the 1995–96 season incorporating a thick green vertical band flanked by white stripes on their blue top, with white sleeves.

Duncan Colquhoun

With the exception of Jack Farrimond, Duncan Colquhoun has been around the club longer than anyone else.

He was on trial with Hibernian when he was told that Wigan Athletic were interested in him. He came down to Springfield Park and was offered a month's trial. He refused and was on the way out of the door when he met the club centre-half, a lad by the name of Hancock, with whom he had been at Millwall. He asked what was going on and when Dunc told him, he went in to see manager Charlie Spencer. What was said remains a mystery, but Charlie Spencer came out of his office and offered Duncan Colquhoun a contract.

He stayed at Latics for a few seasons before club financial problems at the time forced his transfer to Bristol City. He then went to Southport and moved on to Bradford City in 1939.

When the war started, League football was temporarily disrupted and during the next six years, he guested for Blackpool, Rochdale and Partick Thistle.

He returned to Latics after the war as trainer-coach to the team that won the Lancashire Combination Championship. He was also manager at Latics for a short time, taking over the reins early in 1970 before the arrival of Gordon Milne. In fact, during his years with the club, Dunc has done the lot—player, coach, trainer, scout, manager and physiotherapist.

Consecutive Home Games

The Latics played an extraordinary and intense sequence of nine home games in succession during 1971–72.

There was no suggestion of course that these matches were all Northern Premier League fixtures. After playing away at Runcorn on 23 October 1971 and winning 2–1, Latics were involved in the following list of matches at Springfield Park, before visiting Scarborough on 4 December, where they drew 2–2.

Date	Opponents	Competition	Score
25 October	Chorley	Northern Premier League	0–0
30 October	Altrincham	Northern Premier League	0–0
31 October	Hereford United	Herefordshire Cup	1–1
6 November	Rhyl	F.A. Cup	2–1
13 November	Goole Town	Northern Premier League	4–1
20 November	Halifax Town	F.A. Cup	2–1
24 November	Liverpool	Lancashire Senior Cup	0–2
27 November	Bradford Park Avenue	Northern Premier League	1–0
29 November	Skelmersdale	Watney Mann Cup	2–1

Cricketers

The Latics have had just one player who was also a cricketer of real distinction and that was Ken Grieves, the Australian-born all-rounder who was one of Lancashire's longest serving professional cricketers, with 452 first-class appearances to his credit.

Ken Grieves was a middle-order batsman, scoring 22,454 runs at an average of 33.66 with a highest score of 224. He also took 242 wickets with his leg-breaks and googlies. He came to England in 1947 to keep goal for Bury. Ken then kept goal for the Latics in 7 Lancashire Combination games in 1951–52 before playing for Bolton Wanderers and Stockport County.

During the 1968–69 season, Latics were dumped out of the Lancashire Junior Cup by Great Harwood, for whom 'Flat Jack' Simmons, the Lancashire off-spinner, played a great part.

Crowd Trouble

However unwelcome, crowd disturbances are far from a modern phenomenon at major football matches. Behaviour at Springfield Park has usually been of a high standard and though Latic supporters are well-renowned for voicing their opinions at suspect referees, the occasions when their demonstrations boil over beyond the verbal are very rare indeed.

However, one such occasion did take place on 29 September 1962, when Wigan entertained Winsford United at Springfield Park. After 64 minutes play, the referee brought the match to a premature end. He had already awarded 40 free kicks, booked four Wigan players and sent off Bill Bradbury, Latics' inside-left, when he waved his arms in a gesture of resignation and called both teams into the dressing rooms.

His action sparked off angry scenes amongst the 3,782 crowd, which was Latics' biggest of the season, and there was a thirty-minute demonstration outside the main stand by hundreds of fans. The referee had already been buffeted by fans as he strode to the dressing rooms, so he left the ground by a side door with a police escort.

Controversy still raged for weeks after the event about the referee's decision—especially as Latics were losing 2–1 at the time!

Death

There has been one notable instance of a Latics player dying in tragic circumstances during his career with the club.

Don Shaw was one of the finest ball players ever seen at Springfield Park. He was always faced with the problem of synchronising his occupation as an insurance broker with his football at Wigan and he made many sacrifices in his private life to help the Latics out.

His death by drowning while on holiday at Newquay in August 1969 stunned everyone connected with Wigan Athletic F.C.—he was

just over 22 years of age and had been married for just over five months.

The previous season Don had scored what was to be his only Northern Premier League goal, but it proved to be the winner at Chorley in a 2–1 win.

Defeats

Individual Games

The Latics' worst home defeat in a first-class match is 0–5—a scoreline inflicted on us by Bristol Rovers in the Third Division on 26 February 1983 and Chelsea in an F.A. Cup Third Round replay on 26 January 1985.

Away from home our heaviest defeat was the 6–1 beating given to us, again by Bristol Rovers, at Twerton Park on 3 March 1990.

However, the heaviest defeat sustained by a Latics side in a competitive fixture appears to have been a 0–8 annihilation suffered at the hands of Hyde United in 1945–46.

Over a Single Season

Our worst defensive record in terms of defeats suffered in a single season was in 1982–83 when the Latics lost 22 out of 46 Third Division games. Conversely, we only lost 7 Fourth Division games in 1981–82 when gaining promotion to Division Three.

Consecutive Matches without Defeat

Latics' best run of games without defeat in the Football League is 21 and was established in 1981–82 as we successfully challenged for promotion from Division Four. The run began on 25 October 1981 (home v. Scunthorpe United 2–1) and finished with a victory in the return fixture (away v. Scunthorpe United 7–2, the most goals we have scored in a Football League match).

In our non-League days, our best run of games without defeat was a run of 52 unbeaten league games—15 September 1965 to 5 November 1966.

Defensive Records

Wigan Athletic's *best* defensive record in the Football League was established in 1981–82 and helped us to gain promotion to Division Three. We conceded 46 goals in that League season and were beaten in only seven matches.

Our *worst* defensive record in the Football League was in 1982–83 when we let in 72 goals in 46 matches in our first season in the Third Division.

At non-League level, our *best* defensive record was in seasons 1969–70 and 1970–71 (both Northern Premier League) when we let in just 32 goals in campaigns which saw us play 38 and 42 matches respectively. Our *worst* defensive record in non-League football was in 1945–46 when we conceded 116 goals in a 38 match season!

Desegregation

On Saturday 4 May 1991 in the last home game of the season at Springfield Park, members of Bradford City's official supporters club, along with those of their Junior Bantams club and Associate members, viewed the game from the sections of the ground usually reserved for Latics supporters.

Desegregation is the direction all true football fans would like to see the game heading and this game between Latics and Bradford City was the first such game since segregation became compulsory. For the record, Wigan won 3–0 with goals from Griffiths (2, 1 penalty) and Powell.

Directors

In the years immediately following the war, it became increasingly difficult to run a successful non-League side due to escalating wage bills and ground and travelling expenses.

The Latics directors at the time were forced to support the club out of their own pockets, helping to pay wages, rates, gas, electricity and general day to day expenses.

In fact, there was a period when the club advertised for passengers to ride in the team coach, paying a fare related to the distance travelled to help subsidise the travel expenses. And on more than one occasion due to the coach being overbooked, the directors were forced to stand to allow for the paying passengers who had reserved their seat. There was also another occasion when the players wages were made up by a collection from the travelling directors.

Dismissals

Although sendings-off are an all too common feature of the modern game, no one should think that football has ever been immune from them.

In 1962–63, the Cheshire League game against Winsford United at Springfield Park developed into a brawl and the referee, after sending off *Bill Bradbury*, abandoned the game a minute later.

The first Latics player to be sent off in a Football League match was *Colin Methven*. He was dismissed after fouling Bradford City's Hutchings after 70 minutes of Latic's 2–1 defeat at the Valley Parade on 16 February 1980.

Certainly one of the oddest sendings-off was that suffered by Bolton midfielder *Steve Thompson*, in the match at Burnden Park on New Years Day 1986. The referee Ken Walmsley has since admitted that when he sent Thompson off he thought he had already booked him, but it was in fact, *Graham Barrow* the Wigan number 8, who had previously been booked!

Draws

Latics played their greatest number of drawn Football League matches in a single season (14) on five occasions— 1984–85, 1985–86, 1988–89, 1989–90 and 1991–92 and their fewest (9) in 1982–83 and 1990–91.

At non-League level, the Latics greatest number of drawn matches in a season is 15 which occurred in the last three seasons of life in the Northern Premier League. Their fewest number of drawn matches (3) occurred in 1956–57 (Lancashire Combination) and 1964–65 (Cheshire League).

Our highest scoring draw at Football League level is 4–4 which occurred at Scunthorpe United on the last day of the 1980–81 season and at Notts County on the opening day of the 1987–88 season.

The greatest number of drawn matches in a single Latics Cup-tie is two: there have been five occasions when matches have gone to a second replay: Witton Albion (Lancashire Combination Cup 1951–52), Crompton Recs (Lancashire Combination Cup 1955–56), Netherfield, (F.A. Cup 1956–57), Port Vale (F.A. Cup 1969–70) and Morecambe (F.A. Trophy 1972–73).

England Internationals

No players have gained full England international caps while registered with the Wigan club, though the nine players below did play for the Latics after their international career was over.

	Position	Number of Caps
Charlie Spencer	Centre-half	2
Johnny Ball	Wing-half	3
Sam Barkas	Left-back	5
George Eastham	Inside-forward	1
Malcolm Barrass	Centre-half	3
Gordon Milne	Wing-half	14

	Position	Number of Caps
Derek Temple	Winger	1
Larry Lloyd	Centre-half	4
Alan Kennedy	Left-back	2

As you can see, a total of 35 caps, but there wasn't a single goal! The last player to represent an England side while with Wigan is Greg Strong, who played for the England U-15 v. West Germany U-15 at Valley Parade, Bradford City in a 2–2 draw.

Ever-Present

The largest number of ever-presents in a season is 5 in 1977–78 (Ian Gillibrand, Tommy Gore, Joe Hinnigan, John Wilkie and Jeff Wright). They all played in 46 League matches as Latics finished second in their last season in the Northern Premier League. At the time of writing, 33 players have been ever-present with Ian Gillibrand leading the way with six full seasons of football.

Fire

Although the 1952–53 season was a great one in terms of football success, it also brought disaster for the club.

Though Athletic remained a force to be reckoned with, rarely were they out of the first six in the Lancashire Combination, they found it difficult to win the Lancashire Junior Cup, which was the senior non-league cup in those days. However, in 1952–53 under the guidance of Ted Goodier, the coveted trophy was back in the boardroom—it was indeed in the boardroom when the old wooden grandstand was in existence.

The grandstand was totally destroyed by fire early on Thursday morning 30 May 1953. Damage was estimated at £7,000. The stand had a seating capacity of 2,000 of which 500 were upholstered. Two of the cup plinths won by Latics were left in the offices underneath the stand and were also destroyed, though fortunately, earlier that evening the Latics trophies had been taken away from the boardroom by the chairman to display elsewhere. The only item of property which was salvaged being the club's safe, which firemen got out of the offices on rollers.

In all probability the fire cost Latics their chance of League membership at the end of the season, for the flames engulfed not only the spectator facilities, but also the dressing rooms and baths, and despite some enthusiastic fund raising by the club's supporters, it took nearly 12 months to raise sufficient money to build a replacement.

Football Association Challenge Cup

It was the season of 1934–35 that saw the first of what became a legendary beginning of several incredible F.A. Cup runs. With the club successfully coming through the preliminary round, both Scarborough and Hereford United were beaten before Latics were drawn away to Carlisle United in the first round proper. The Wigan fans travelled in their droves over the Cumbrian border to see Latics crush United by 6–1 with goals from Armes (2), Roberts (2), Scott and Robson. In the second round, Latics humbled Torquay United 3–2 in front of an ecstatic Springfield Park crowd of 20,003. The Lions of Millwall were the next to visit Springfield Park, with a near record attendance of 25,304 watching the game in which the visitors won 4–1.

In 1953–54, Scarborough were the first team to reel under the strength of the rampant Wigan side, going down 4–0 at Springfield Park in front of 12,692 spectators. The draw for the second round pitched the club at home again against one of the South's top non-League clubs—Hereford United. A record crowd of 27,526 spectators watched as Latics won 4–1. Athletic were rewarded for this victory with an away draw at St James's Park with the mighty Newcastle

Paul Jewell shows his delight in scoring the goal in our 1–0 defeat of first division Norwich City.

United, the premier club in football. The Latics stunned the soccer world by holding Milburn and his men 2–2 before a crowd of 52,222. Sadly, Wigan lost the replay 3–2.

In 1970–71, the Latics, then managed by Gordon Milne, fought their way through to the Third Round yet again, defeating League opposition in Peterborough United on the way. They were rewarded with a draw at Maine Road to play high-flying Manchester City. Wigan again captured the hearts of the football nation with a stunning display of football but a goal scored by Colin Bell just over ten minutes from the end put paid to their giant-killing hopes.

However, whenever the subject of giant-killing comes up, then the name of Wigan Athletic will always be mentioned first. The number of League clubs knocked out of the Cup in Latics' non-League days is impressive—Carlisle United, Doncaster Rovers, Peterborough United, Halifax Town, Shrewsbury, Hereford United, Southport, York City and Sheffield Wednesday.

In 1979–80, Latics second season as a Football League club, they had their most successful season to date in the F.A. Cup competition, reaching the Fourth Round. They beat Blackpool 2–0 after a 1–1 draw, Northwich Victoria 1–0 after a 2–2 draw and an opening game which saw Latics leading 3–0 until the game was abandoned due to fog, and Chelsea 1–0 at Stamford Bridge, before going down 3–0 at Everton.

In 1986–87, the Latics embarked on a glorious Cup run, knocking First Division Norwich City out along the way before Leeds United rode their luck to go through in the 6th round tie played at Springfield Park.

Latic's complete F.A. Cup record to the end of the 1994–95 season is as follows:

P	W	D	L	F	A
198	99	43	56	377	242

F.A. Challenge Trophy

For a number of years the F.A. was under pressure to organise a new Cup competition especially for non-League professional clubs who, once out of the F.A. Cup, had no second trophy to aim for. Accordingly, in 1967 the Association enquired of what support a knock-out Cup competition for non-League clubs would receive and were overwhelmed with the response. The F.A. Council formally approved the organisation of the F.A. Challenge Trophy in September 1968 and some 200 entries were received for the first competition in season 1969–70.

Macclesfield Town were the initial winners when they beat Telford United 2–0, but it did not take long for the losers to go one better. The following year in fact, they re-appeared in the final and defeated Hillingdon Borough 3–2, although at half-time they were trailing by two goals. In 1971–72, Stafford Rangers overcame Barnet by three clear goals.

The following season will always be remembered as Wigan's Wembley Year, as a fantastic run in the F.A. Challenge Trophy earned them a place in the final.

In the run to Wembley, the first F.A. Trophy finalists to have been closely related to a former member of the Football League, beat Burton Albion 5–0, South Liverpool 2–0 and Romford 2–0. The Fourth Round was a marathon—300 minutes of football; 1–1 at Morecambe, 0–0 at Wigan and 1–0 at Blackburn in the second replay. That put the Latics in the semi-final. They were drawn against Stafford at Port

F.A. CHALLENGE TROPHY COMPETITION

FINAL

SCARBOROUGH

VERSUS

WIGAN
ATHLETIC

SATURDAY, 28th APRIL, 1973   Kick-off 3 p.m.

WEMBLEY

 EMPIRE   STADIUM

OFFICIAL PROGRAMME 10p

 *The programme for the F. A. Challenge Trophy Final, when despite a
John Rogers goal we lost 1–2 after extra time.*

 Action from the Wembley defeat.

Vale's ground, but the game finished a goalless draw and there was a further replay at Oldham—Wigan were successful 1–0, a goal scored by Graham Oates—WIGAN WERE WEMBLEY BOUND.

Almost 19,000 tickets were sold in Wigan for this Wembley final—the actual attendance being 24,000. Wigan's opponents that day were Scarborough.

It had been a long season, with over sixty games played and it showed in Latics' play. Just 11 minutes into the game, Scarborough scored through Leask. They defended stoutly, but Wigan deserved their equaliser, although they almost left it too late. John Rogers' shot from 20 yards somehow found its way through half a dozen players and then through the goalkeeper's legs—just 15 seconds from time! The game had to go into extra-time, but four minutes from the final whistle, Thompson hit Scarborough's second goal. There were no last minute comebacks and so Latics finished with losers medals.

It was a great achievement to reach the final however and as the team returned to Wigan on the Sunday, they were given a tremendous welcome and a Civic Reception in the Town Hall.

Jack Farrimond

Jack Farrimond was connected with Wigan Athletic since its formation in 1932.

As a boy, he watched the defunct Wigan Borough. His father was one of Latics' first directors and a life vice-president. In 1932, Jack Farrimond became Latics' first secretary, a post he held until 1936, when he left the club to take up the post of rate collector for the Wigan Corporation, which he did with some sadness. Indeed, manager Charlie Spencer who also owned a confectionery shop in Blackpool was foremost in organising Jack's honeymoon during a very busy August Bank Holiday week. As a club director, Jack Farrimond worked tirelessly on behalf of the Latics, though during the war years he served in the R.A.F.

In 1948 he took over the position of secretary again until 1953 when he was asked to become the Supporters Club financial secretary. He held this position until 1968 when he returned to the board.

Employed as a welfare home superintendent with Wigan Corporation, he was also a Lancashire Football Association Council member. It was he who originated the idea of a national non-league to act as a feeder to the Football League.

Until his recent death, he was a life vice-president of the Latics.

Jack Farrimond.

Floodlights

In 1966–67 Latics won five trophies, including the Northern Floodlight League and Knockout Cup and the Lancashire F.A. Floodlight Cup. Wigan's entry into the world of floodlight competitions was new, thanks to the installation of the Springfield Park lights, which were switched on at the start of that season when Manchester City were the guests in front of a 10,000 crowd.

Football League

Wigan Athletic were elected to the Football League on Friday 2 June 1978, after thirty-five disappointing rejections.

We played our first Football League match at Hereford United on 19 August 1978, drawing 0–0 in an impressive League début. In each of our first three seasons in the League, we made challenging runs but were unable to sustain our form enough to earn promotion, which was eventually achieved in 1981–82.

The statistics from our opening two league campaigns are interesting though, the final figures being almost identical as you can see and although the number of goals are different, the goal difference remained the same +15.

Season	League Position	P	W	D	L	F	A	Pts
1978–79	6th	46	21	13	12	63	48	55
1979–80	6th	46	21	13	12	76	61	55

The Latics won promotion in 1981–82, taking third place behind Bradford City and Sheffield United. Their tally of 91 points (3 points for a win) remains their highest in the Football League.

In their first three seasons in Division Three, they finished 18th, 15th and 16th respectively. In 1985–86 they finished fourth, missing

promotion by just one point, whilst the following season they earned a play-off place only to go down 3–2 to Swindon Town on aggregate.

In 1987–88, the club finished seventh in Division Three, though after their 2–1 victory at Walsall in September, they went top. The following season saw Latics struggle in the lower reaches, their best season being 1990–91 when they finished tenth.

Football League Cup

Sad to relate, the Latics have failed to make much impact on the Football League (later Milk, Littlewoods, Rumblelows and Coca Cola) Cup.

Latics' *best performance* in the Football League has been to reach the last sixteenth (fourth round) in 1981–82. We defeated Stockport

 Mark Hilditch cracks home another goal in the 5–0 win over Wrexham on 29 August 1989.

County, Aldershot and Chelsea, before going out at home to Aston Villa 2–1, though at half-time we led through a Peter Houghton goal.

The club's *best scoreline* in the League Cup was the 5–0 victory over Wrexham in a 1st Round (2nd leg) tie here at Springfield Park on 29 August 1989, but few will argue that our *best result* was the 4–2 defeat of Chelsea in the 3rd round of our most successful season, when 12,063 saw Mark Wignall (2), Clive Evans and Les Bradd score the Latics' goals. Though when we played Liverpool at Anfield on 19 September 1989 in the 2nd Round (1st leg—both ties were played at Anfield) we amazingly led 2–1 for ten minutes, despite going a goal behind inside four minutes. Bryan Griffiths and Dave Thompson were the players to send the Wigan fans wild!

Bobby Campbell who scored all three in our 3–1 win at Burnden Park in the 1st round (2nd leg) in 1987–88 after Bolton had won 3–2 at Springfield Park, is the only player to score a hat-trick for Latics in the League Cup.

Latics' record to date in the League Cup is as follows:

P	W	D	L	F	A
55	16	12	27	68	88

Foreign Opponents

In 1969–70, the Latics entertained Metallist of Khartrov from Russia in what was the first friendly match against foreign opponents. Despite goals from Sutherland and Fleming, the Latics went down 3–2 in front of a 3,992 crowd. This is the game where the assistant secretary of Khartrov was Mikhail Gorbachev—now a Latics fan!

We fared no better five seasons later, going down by the same score at home to Moscow Torpedo.

Our first victory against foreign opposition came in our first season in the Football League, when thanks to goals by Seddon and Purdie (pen) we beat S.P.Erkenschwick of Germany 2–1.

The Latics' highest scoring encounter with foreign opposition came the following season when Tulsa Roughnecks were defeated 4–3. We

Jimmy Carberry nips in between Sergei Zhukov and Valentin Kovack to start another Latics attack.

later visited Malta, losing 2–1 to Floriana, for whom the then Wigan director, Bobby Charlton played.

Our next visitors were CWKs Legia Warsaw from Poland, who beat us 3–0 in a fairly one-sided affair. In 1981–82, we entertained Bodo Grad from Norway and won 4–2 with Wright (2), Butler and Mick Quinn getting the Latics' goals. This time, Bobby Charlton turned out for the Latics game against the Norwegians, who were managed by the ex-Latics assistant manager, Chris Lawler.

Moscow Torpedo visited Springfield Park for a second time in 1989–90, playing out a goalless draw in front of 2,255 spectators.

Our visit to the USSR in 1990–91 saw us lose both games, 2–1 to Dynamo Brest (Griffiths getting the Latics goal) and 4–1 to Brest Select XI (David Fairclough netting for Wigan). The last game involving foreign opponents at Springfield Park came in the same season when Dynamo Brest provided the opposition. A crowd of only 841 saw Latics triumph 3–1 with goals from Page (2) and Rimmer.

We have also entertained two national sides at Springfield Park. We defeated Zambia 2–1 in 1978–79, whilst four seasons later we drew 1–1 against China, with John Rogers getting our goal.

Fourth Division

The 2 June 1978 will always be remembered by Wigan Athletic fans, being the day when, after many years of frustration, the club realised its ambition by being elected to Associate Membership of the Football League. The club spent four seasons in the League basement before gaining promotion to Division Three by finishing in third place behind Sheffield United and Bradford City in 1981–82 with 91 points. It was the first season of three points for a win and is Latics' highest total for a season in League football.

Our Fourth Division record reads as follows:

P	W	D	L	F	A
184	86	50	48	270	210

Freight Rover Trophy Final

On Saturday 1 June 1985, Wigan Athletic won the first ever Freight Rover Trophy Final. It was the first time the Associate Members of the Football League had their own Wembley Final.

Brentford 1 Wigan Athletic 3

Goals from Mike Newell, Tony Kelly and David Lowe killed off the challenge of gallant Brentford in a match that will live long in the memories of the 39,897 who saw it.

The Latics, outnumbered off the field by fans who could virtually walk to the stadium, made up for that with an almost faultless display. Goalkeeper Tunks had done well in the early stages when all the defenders also worked hard, but Wigan got on top and the first goal came in the 25th minute. Barry Knowles, only in the team because of injury to John Butler, looped a ball to the right for Mike Newell to control and crash a great shot into the net. The second goal came 12

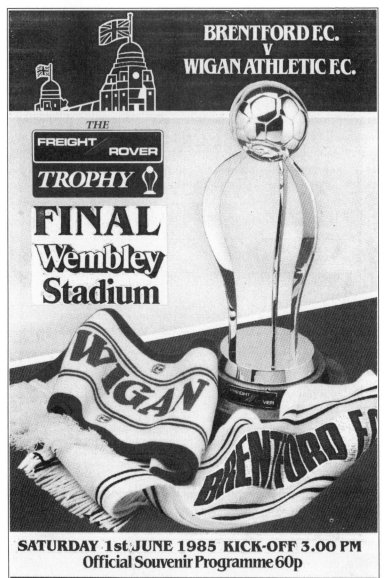

The programme for the Freight Rover trophy final on 1 June 1985 when we beat Brentford 3–1.

 Latics and Brentford take the field before the FRT final.

minutes later when Graham Barrow back-heeled the ball for Tony Kelly to beat the Brentford 'keeper with a well struck long shot.

There was a shock for the Latics soon after the re-start when Cooke scored for Brentford with a super volley. Fortunately Wigan hit back and Newell was unlucky to have a shot cleared off the line. From the resulting corner, David Lowe scored a spectacular third goal for Latics with an overhead kick from a pass by Gary Bennett.

The final whistle confirmed what all Latics' fans had known for the majority of the second half—that the Freight Rover Trophy was on its way to Springfield Park.

Friendlies

Perhaps Latics' *most unusual friendly* was played in February 1960 when the club chartered a plane to fly to play Stirling Albion in

Mike Newell heads for goal in the FRT final v. *Brentford.*

Scotland. This didn't go as hoped as they lost 5–1 and the trip home became a saga when the plane broke down and the party were forced to hitch home on separate flights as they became available.

Other friendlies that come to mind are the visit of Grimsby Town at the end of the 1949–50 season, when the Latics with Tom Finney guesting went down 3–5 in front of 16,000; the defeat by Flint Town United in the Festival of Britain in 1950–51 by 3–1 with Tolley (pen) getting the Latics goal, and the 2–1 win over St Mirren the following season when Nat Lofthouse, Johnny Ball and Malcolm Barrass from Bolton Wanderers guested for the Latics.

When Latics entertained Everton in 1958–59, the side also included four guest players—Les Campbell (Preston North End), Bill Eckersley (Blackburn Rovers), Simm (Bradford City) and Newman (Yorkshire League trialist)—the result a 5–2 win for the visitors. In 1967–68, Latics entertained Port Vale (3–3). The Vale side included 52-year-old Stanley Matthews. Vale were later expelled from the Football League after making illegal payments. They were reinstated the following month.

Larry Lloyd's team started the 1981–82 season off by playing a remarkable nine pre-season friendlies—it must have worked, for at the end of the season, we gained promotion!

Goalkeepers

Wigan Athletic F.C. has almost always been extremely well served by its goalkeepers and most of them have been highly popular with our supporters. Many names spring to mind, such as Bert Lomas of the famous Ted Goodier side, Harold Woolley, Harry Sharratt, Dave Gaskell, Dennis Reeves and Roy Tunks.

Harold Woolley performed heroically between the sticks when Latics won the Lancashire Combination in their first season. They got off to a poor start though, as did Woolley. He let in five goals as Latics lost their first match in the Combination 1–5 at home to Fleetwood.

A local pit man, Woolley became a great favourite with the crowd. On one occasion, Latics lost a cup-tie at Marine. The second goal which killed off the Latics, came as a result of a misunderstanding between Woolley and captain Jimmy Shirley. After the game, Woolley was seen sitting on his haunches on his doorstep by a Latics fan, 'I should have caught that ball, shouldn't I?' inquired the 'keeper. 'Never mind,' said the supporter, 'it couldn't be helped.'

'Couldn't be helped,' snapped Woolley, 'if Shirley had left me to it I could have taken the ...... lace out of the thing, never mind caught it.'

Harry Sharratt signed for Latics in 1948 as an amateur and he kept his amateur status throughout his career. Wigan were just one of many clubs who tried to persuade Harry to turn professional, but he resisted all temptation because he wanted to remain a schoolteacher and also play for England at amateur level. He stayed with Latics 'on and off' for about three seasons, but in the meantime, he had spells with Bishop Auckland. It was while playing for 'The Bishops' that he was capped for England.

Dennis Reeves was signed from Wrexham in the late 1960s and quickly established himself in the first team. He was a firm favourite

with the Latics fans, who admired his solid, dependable performances. After signing for Latics, Dennis Reeves played in a number of successful teams and gave many memorable performances, not least against Manchester City in 1971 when he pulled off some tremendous saves before, ironically, his boot split while taking a goal-kick and the ball fell to a City player who set up the winning goal for Colin Bell. His performance in the F.A. Challenge Trophy semi-final replay against Stafford Rangers at Boundary Park, helped Latics win 1–0 and Dennis played at Wembley against Scarborough, in what was probably his proudest moment.

Goalscoring

For the club

The Latics' highest goalscoring tally was achieved in 1986–87 when the team that finished fourth in Division Three and lost in the play-offs, scored 83 League goals in 46 matches. Our best season in non-League football was 1934–35 when we scored 153 goals in winning the Cheshire League Championship.

By the individual

The following players have scored 80 or more goals for the club:

Player		Goals
Harry Lyon	1962–69	273
Billy Lomax	1949–55	189
Bert Llewellyn	1965–68	147
Horace Thomas	1932–40	132
John Rogers	1972–84	125
Jackie Lyon	1950–55	122
Micky Worswick	1972–78	112

Player		*Goals*
George Scott	1933–36	102
Edward T. Felton	1933–36	98
Roy Smith	1955–59	89
Peter Houghton	1977–84	88
Jack Livesey	1952–55	84

In the Football League our top ten goalscorers are:

Peter Houghton	1978–84	62
Bryan Griffiths	1988–93	52
David Lowe	1982–87	40
Phil Daley	1989–94	39
Graham Barrow	1981–86	36
Paul Jewell	1984–88	35
Bobby Campbell	1986–88	27

 Phil Daley.

 David Lowe (above) and Mike Newell (below).

Player		Goals
Mark Hilditch	1986–90	26
Les Bradd	1981–83	25
Mike Newell	1983–86	25
Eamonn O'Keefe	1982–83	25

Key: All dates refer to the calendar years of débuts and last appearances.
Correct to August 1995.

Ted Goodier

Ted Goodier was brought to Wigan Athletic by the then chairman, Sid Littler, at the start of the 1952–53 season and, in the seasons that followed, Latics' trophy room was almost permanently filled.

One thing that is not remembered about this colourful character is that he was no mean player. A big, tough wing-half, Ted Goodier was once asked who in his mind was the best. 'Stanley Matthews', he replied, 'I played against him, but he only got past me once—the next time he came along, he went over the railings!'

When he came to the club, Ted Goodier kept just two players, left-back Harry Parkinson and inside-forward Jackie Lyon, but he proceeded to build up a tremendous line-up that was to rule the world of non-League football.

A big man, standing more than six feet tall, Ted Goodier was the strictest of disciplinarians. The players knew exactly where they stood and not one of them ever put a foot out of line for they had the highest respect for their boss.

In the famous season of 1953–54, Latics won practically everything there was to win—the Lancashire Combination Championship, the Lancashire Junior Cup and the Makerfield Cup. In fact, they had gone one better the previous year, when they scooped all that little lot, plus the Lancashire Combination Cup, but I suppose the F.A. Cup run culminating with Newcastle United made the 1953–54 season more memorable.

Ted Goodier stayed with the Latics until 1956, when a personal row with Sid Littler, the man who had brought him to Springfield Park, led to him being sacked.

He wasn't out of a job for long though, taking over at Oldham Athletic soon after his surprise dismissal by the Latics.

Ted Goodier was the father-figure behind the team development which was to make Wigan Athletic's post-Second World War reputation as an elite non-League club.

Mikhail Gorbachev

Latics' first meeting with foreign opponents was in 1969–70 when Metallist of Khartrov of Russia visited Springfield Park, winning an exciting game 3–2.

The assistant secretary of Metallist of Khartrov was a certain Mikhail Gorbachev. The former Soviet President was reported to follow the fixtures of Latics thereafter, as he enjoyed his visit so much!

Guest Players

The 'guest' system was used by all clubs during the war. Although at times it was abused almost beyond belief, it normally worked sensibly and effectively, to the benefit of players, clubs and supporters alike.

However, it was in friendly matches after the war that distinguished players 'guested' for the Latics.

At the end of the 1949–50 season, Latics with Tom Finney guesting played Grimsby Town in a friendly (3–5) in front of 16,000 spectators. Against St Mirren in 1951–52, three Bolton players, Nat Lofthouse, Johnny Ball (ex-Latics) and Malcolm Barrass all 'guested' as Wigan won 2–1 with Barrass scoring the winning goal. The latter two became Wigan managers.

In the friendly game against Floriana in Malta in 1979–80, the then Latics director, Bobby Charlton turned out for Floriana. However,

Bobby turned out for the Latics a few seasons later in the game against Bodo Grad, who were managed by the ex-Latics assistant manager, Chris Lawler.

Bryan Hamilton

A terrier-like midfielder in his playing days with Linfield, Ipswich Town, Everton, Millwall, Swindon and Tranmere Rovers, he won 50 caps for Northern Ireland.

In October 1980 he joined Tranmere as their player-manager and though he made his final appearance in November 1983, he remained in charge at Prenton Park until February 1985 when he was sacked.

Joining Wigan Athletic he led the club to fourth place in Division Three and to a Freight Rover Trophy Final victory in May 1985. He joined Leicester City in June 1986 but the Filberts were relegated and when struggling the following season he was sacked.

Upon his return to Springfield Park he had rather an ambiguous role and only took full charge of team affairs in March 1989. Struggling with low crowds and little success on the pitch, Hamilton still managed to keep the side in the Third Division for four seasons which was a miracle in itself.

In March 1993 he lost his job as the club struggled to get away from the bottom of the table. The one bright spot of Hamilton's last season was Wigan reaching the Northern Final of the Autoglass Trophy where they lost at Stockport County and missed out on a trip to Wembley.

Hat-tricks

There have been three occasions in our non-League days when two Latics players have scored hat-tricks in the same match.

Corfield (4) and *Vincent* (3) scored in the 12–0 Lancashire Combination Cup victory over Stubshaw Cross in 1954–55; the following

season, *W. McLean* and *Smith* scored three each in our 9–2 victory over Prescot Cables in the same competition, and in 1957–58, *Hitchen* and *Smith* also hit three each in the 10–1 rout of Crompton Recs in the Makerfield Cup.

There have been two occasions when a player has scored a double hat-trick. The first came in the Lancashire Junior Cup of 1958–59 when *Taberner* scored six goals in our 7–2 away win at Crompton Recs. In 1969–70, *Tony McLoughlin* scored seven goals in our 11–1 Lancashire Challenge Trophy victory over Darwen.

The club's first hat-trick in the Football League came from *Peter Houghton* in the home match with Port Vale in 1978–79—his goals all coming in the space of ten minutes. Houghton also had the distinction of scoring Latics' first hat-trick away from Springfield Park in the 3–2 win at Tranmere Rovers in 1980–81, and along with *Eamonn O'Keefe*, holds the record for the most hat-tricks (3) in the Football League. Latics' last league hat-trick was scored by *David Thompson* at Shrewsbury Town on Tuesday 20 March 1990 in a 3–1 win. The last hat-trick at home in the league was on Monday 1 January 1990 when Latics beat Mansfield Town 4–0 with *Mark Hilditch* getting three goals and Thompson the other. The last player to score a hat-trick at Springfield Park was *Don Page* in Wigan's 4–0 Leyland DAF Cup win over Chester City on 6 November 1990.

In 1937–38, *Duncan Colquhoun's* hat-trick in the 7–0 F.A. Cup triumph over Lytham St Annes was an historic first. Only two other players have scored them since, *Ronnie Barker* (on two occasions) and the legendary *Harry Lyon* (three times).

Hereford United

Hereford United and Wigan Athletic have quite a lot in common. For many years they were non-League clubs aspiring to become members of the Football League. In 1971, the Herefordshire F.A. chose by invitation Wigan Athletic as Hereford's County Cup Final opponents—the game at Springfield Park ended 1–1 whilst Hereford scored the only goal of the game at Edgar Street.

UNITED

THE OFFICIAL MATCH MAGAZINE OF HEREFORD UNITED

 1.5p

Wigan Athletic

FOOTBALL LEAGUE
FOURTH DIVISION

on AUGUST 19th

MATCH SPONSORED BY RENWICKS MOTORS

1978~79 SEASON

 The programme for Latics first ever Football League match at Hereford United on 19 August 1978.

In December 1953, the Latics drew Hereford United in the F.A. Cup Second Round at Springfield Park. This game provided a record gate for two non-League clubs (outside Wembley) of 27,526, and it is doubtful if this will ever be beaten. Wigan won this game 4–1 and were drawn against Newcastle United in the Third Round at St James' Park.

Finally, when Wigan became members of the Football League in 1978, our first League fixture was at Hereford, where we drew 0–0. On that occasion, Mr P.S. Hill presented the Wigan chairman with a statue of the famous Herefordshire Bull. This ornament is a coveted possession displayed in the board room.

Home Matches

Latics' best home wins were the 12–0 rout of Stubshaw Cross in a 1954–55 Lancashire Combination Cup match, the 12–1 win over Congleton Town in the 1937–38 Cheshire League match, the 11–0 victory over Witton Albion in the 1934–35 Cheshire League fixture and the 11–1 Lancashire Challenge Trophy win over Darwen in 1969–70 when Tony McLoughlin scored 7 goals. We scored double figures at home on three other occasions: 10–1 against Chester Reserves (Cheshire League 1934–35), Earlestown (Lancashire Junior Cup 1953–54) and Crompton Recs (Mackereth Cup 1957–58).

Wigan's worst home defeat is 0–5 against Bristol Rovers on 26 February 1983 (Division 3) and Chelsea on 26 January 1985 (F.A. Cup Third Round replay), though we did concede six goals in a 3–6 defeat at home to Northwich Victoria in the 1946–47 Cheshire League season.

Home Seasons

Wigan Athletic have gone through a League season at non-League level with an undefeated home record on five occasions. They were:

1933–34   Cheshire League when we won all 21 matches.
1934–35   Cheshire League we won 19 and drew 2.
1952–53   Lancashire Combination we won 16 and drew 5.
1965–66   Cheshire League we won 17 and drew 4.
1969–70   Northern Premier League we won 13 and drew 6.

The nearest we came to it at Football League level was 1981–82 when we lost only one home game, 0–1 to Sheffield United in our opening home game of the season.

Joseph Howarth

Joseph Howarth presided over 'The Magnificent Seven', the committee who brought about the formation of Latics, and then when the football club became a limited company in January 1933, he was appointed its first chairman. It was a position he was to hold for the first four years of the club's life. His excellent business sense and qualities of leadership got the club off to exactly the right kind of start with the right kind of foundations.

Joseph Howarth's record outside the world of football was just as impressive. A magistrate, he joined the board of management of the Hindley Industrial Co-operative as far back as 1896 and was that body's president for a remarkable fifty-one years—at that time a national record.

From the day of Wigan Athletic's formation, Joseph Howarth's enthusiasm for the club never wavered and he remained chairman until retiring in 1946. On his retirement, he was made president and held that position until his death at the age of eighty-one in January 1951.

There is no doubt that football in Wigan owes a great debt of gratitude to this great personality.

Isle of Man Festival

Prior to the start of the 1986–87 season, Latics were involved in the Isle of Man Festival. Playing in Group 'B', the Latics finished top to qualify for the final. Their results in Group 'B' were:

Opponents	Venue	Score	Scorers
Bohemians	Ramsey	4–1	Butler, I. Griffiths, C. Thompson, Jewell
Hearts	Douglas	1–1	Lowe
Stoke City	Ramsey	1–0	I. Griffiths

In the final at Douglas, the Latics beat Portsmouth 1–0 after extra time, with David Lowe grabbing the all-important goal.

Junior Latics

The first meeting of the Junior Latics on 7 September 1981 was a very special occasion. Almost 300 children and parents packed into the Wigan Athletic Supporters Club for what must be one of the most memorable evenings it has ever seen.

The guest list was like a who's who of Wigan Athletic Football Club with Junior Latics' president Bobby Charlton, C.B.E., manager Larry Lloyd, club chairman Freddie Pye, captain Colin Methven, members of the board of directors and members of the playing staff.

Almost fourteen years later, the club is as strong as ever.

Lancashire Combination

The first competitive season after the war was probably one of the best in the history of the club. After failing to gain re-election to the Cheshire League, the club along with Accrington Stanley, entered the Lancashire Combination.

After a disastrous start (losing 5–1 at home to Fleetwood) Duncan Colquhoun, a star of the 1930s team returned to Springfield Park to build virtually from scratch, a purely local side that astounded everyone by winning the league at their first attempt.

The final table read:

	P	W	D	L	F	A	Pts
Wigan Athletic	42	25	9	8	72	37	59
Nelson	42	24	9	9	84	67	57

Over the following seasons, Athletic proved themselves to be formidable opponents, holding almost a monopolistic grip on the Lancashire Combination championship title.

It went to Latics in the 1950–51 season and then again in 1952–53. The following season was one of the most remarkable in Wigan's 60-year history. They not only retained the championship (the third in four years) of the Lancashire Combination League, but also won the Lancashire Junior Cup and Lancashire Combination Cup.

The following years were uneventful and in many respects the club was heading towards stagnation, having really outgrown the Lancashire Combination.

During the 1960–61 season, the management of the club became all too aware of the general stagnation of both the club and the League in which they were competing, and applied to join the Cheshire League where football was altogether stronger and the competition fiercer.

Latics' full record in the Lancashire Combination is as follows:

P	W	D	L	F	A	Pts
578	315	114	149	1241	769	744

Largest Crowd

It was on 12 January 1929 that Springfield Park housed its largest crowd. The occasion was the F.A. Cup Third Round match between Wigan Borough and Sheffield Wednesday. The crowd was 30,611, the receipts £1,800 (the admission price was only 1 shilling then) as the visitors ran out winners by 3–1.

The largest crowd to watch Wigan Athletic at Springfield Park was 27,526 when Hereford United were the visitors on 12 December 1953.

Last-Kick No-Goal!

There is always one incident which stands out when the name of Alf Craig, one of the most popular centre-halves ever to put on the Wigan Athletic shirt, is mentioned amongst Latic supporters—the famous 'no-goal' incident against Tranmere Rovers in 1966.

The setting was a first round F.A. Cup replay at Springfield Park, played in a blinding snow storm. Latics had made an excellent draw at Prenton Park on the previous Saturday and a huge crowd was present to see the replay. The League side were winning by the only goal of the game, when, in the dying seconds, Alf fired in a terrific shot that almost broke the back of the Tranmere net. The Wigan fans went wild; some thinking that Latics had equalised, but others because the referee had disallowed the goal, claiming he had blown for full-time before the ball entered the net.

A cruel story was passed around after the match that the referee had a 10 o'clock train to catch and did not want to miss it by playing extra time!

Last Matches

Latics last ever matches in the Lancashire Combination, Cheshire League and Northern Premier League were all away from home, but were all won.

Lancashire Combination: 4 May 1961 *v.* Earlestown 3–0
Cheshire League: 4 May 1968 *v.* Oswestry Town 2–1
Northern Premier League: 5 May 1978 *v.* Matlock Town 1–0

Last Minute Goals

The season of 1991–92 saw a run of three games where Wigan conceded a last minute goal in each—Hartlepool United (a 3–4), Reading (h 1–1) and Birmingham City (a 3–3).

Perhaps the most frantic finish to a Latics game also came this season in the home game against Darlington. Latics' Gary Powell equalised in the 89th minute, only to see Darlington re-take the lead in the 90th minute.

Late Finishes to a Season

Latics' victory over Brentford in the Freight Rover Trophy Final at Wembley on Saturday 1 June 1985 is the latest date for the finish of any Latics season. In 1987, the club were involved in the play-offs against Swindon Town with both matches being played in mid-May.

League Record

Since Latics' entry into the Football League at the beginning of the 1978–79 season, their full league record to the end of the 1994–95 season is as follows:

	P	W	D	L	F	A	Pts
Home	387	196	90	101	609	404	638
Away	387	101	116	170	441	603	398
Total	774	297	206	271	1050	1007	1036

Home Wins—40 at 2 points   156 at 3 points

Away Wins—20 at 2 points   81 at 3 points

Larry Lloyd

A dominant figure in the centre of defence, Larry Lloyd's spells at Liverpool and Nottingham Forest coincided with some vintage years for both clubs. He scored one of the goals in Liverpool's UEFA Cup Final win over Borussia Moenchengladbach in 1973 and appeared in two European successes for Forest. He won four full caps for England and League championship medals at both Anfield and the City ground.

Though he was not successful as a manager, he led Wigan Athletic to promotion to Division Three in 1981–82 but was sacked the following season.

Billy Lomax

One of the best remembered players ever to don a Latics shirt, Billy Lomax was a discovery of Army football.

On his demob, he joined Lancashire Combination side Netherfield and made a sensational début, scoring four goals. He scored 14 goals for Netherfield in just seven matches before stepping into League football with Carlisle United. He stayed at Brunton Park until 1946 when he joined Macclesfield Town. In his stay with the Silkmen which lasted two and a half seasons, he scored 90 goals.

Billy Lomax joined Latics in the 1949–50 season and that campaign scored 42 goals. The following season he netted 54 times and registered 11 goals in 1951–52 before he was transferred to Nelson.

It was in his second spell with Latics that Billy really hit the goalscoring heights. Signed by Ted Goodier at the beginning of the 1952–53 season, he scored 35 goals, whilst the following season he was joint top scorer with Jackie Lyon and Jack Livesey when each player scored a staggering 40 goals.

Though he worked at Bickershaw Colliery as a coalminer, goals were Billy's business and while he was in his second spell with Latics he set up records galore.

In October 1953, he scored five goals against Hyde United in a match at Ewans Fields and thus became the first man in Latics' history to score 150 goals for the first team.

Billy was a member of the famous F.A. Cup side that played Newcastle United at St James' Park and it is that match which throws out a delightful story about Billy Lomax.

As the Wigan team were in the dressing room before the game, the door opened and the Magpies' giant centre-half Frank Brennan walked in and said, 'Who's your centre-forward?' Billy stood up and said, 'I am. Why?' To which Brennan retorted, 'You had better get ready because you are not going to even see the ball today.' At the end of the game, Brennan came to Billy, shook his hand and said, 'I've never played in a game like that, you were great.'

Billy Lomax's career with Wigan Athletic ended in 1954 and he left Springfield Park failing by only 14 goals to record a double century for the first team.

Long Service

Kenny Banks and Duncan Colquhoun are both so well known to Latics' fans that their careers are like an open book.

'Banksey' is the more familiar of the two because he has run onto the pitch every week for many years past to tend to Wigan's injured players. He has a permanent place in the hearts of Latics fans because he was a member of the Wigan side that took the mighty Newcastle United to two games in the 1950s. 'Dunc' like Kenny Banks is still remembered with great affection by the older Latics fans. Now in his seventies, 'Dunc' celebrated a 50-year association with the club.

When Ian Gillibrand opened up the 1978–79 season with Wigan Athletic, he began his 12th season as a Latics first team player; Harry Parkinson and Derek Houghton both played 10 seasons for the club whilst Kevin Langley who started his career in 1981–82 holds the record for the most League appearances for the club.

Of course, Latics' most loyal servant is Jack Farrimond who became Wigan secretary in 1932 and was at the time of his death, a life vice-president of the club.

Lowest

The lowest number of goals scored by Wigan Athletic in a single Football League season is the 43 in 1992–93 in Division Two. At non-League level, our lowest is 56 in 1969–70 when we finished as runners-up in the Northern Premier League.

Our lowest points record in the Football League also occurred in 1992–93 when we gained 41 points, whilst in our non-League days, the season of 1946–47 saw us amass just 25 points to finish bottom of the Cheshire League.

Harry Lyon

Harry Lyon was perhaps the finest goalscorer ever to wear a Latics shirt. He holds the record for the most goals in a season—67—a figure that will surely never be beaten. He was as deadly a finishing centre-forward as one could find in non-League football at the time he was playing.

Signed from Burscough by Allan Brown in 1965, he began to hit the net straight away and the fans knew that the manager had brought a player of rare quality into the team.

Equally deadly with both feet and head, Harry was a big, bustling centre-forward in the old mould who would 'run through a brick wall' if it meant scoring a goal. But of all the 273 goals he did score, there are three from Harry that stand out in the memory. All were scored in the same match and it was an F.A. Cup-tie against Doncaster Rovers which no Latics fan will ever forget.

It was the 1965–66 season when Latics entertained Doncaster in a replay after coming away from Yorkshire with a magnificent draw. Things looked black for Wigan when Harry Lyon was injured just before half-time and had to be carried from the field on a stretcher with what appeared to be a severe leg injury.

After half-time however, Harry reappeared on the touchline, swathed in bandages and to quote his own words 'with half a bottle of whisky inside'. The cheers when he came back on the field could be heard in Doncaster; the cheers as he proceeded to score a hat-trick could be heard much farther afield. Latics finally won 3–1 and Harry Lyon became a Springfield Park immortal.

He stayed at Springfield through the reign of Allan Brown and when Ian McNeill arrived for his first stint as manager, he was switched to centre-half for a time. In fact, in his later years, he played in nearly every position for the team, even in goal when needed!

Harry's illustrious career was coming to an end when Ian McNeill took over and he was released at the end of the 1969–70 season. He moved to Chorley, but never really settled at Victory Park and the career of a superb goalscorer came to an end in the early 1970s.

Managers

This is the complete list of Latics managers, with the inclusive dates in which they held office. Biographies of those who have made major contributions to the club are included in alphabetical order in this A–Z.

Charlie Spencer	1932–37	Alf Craig	1966–67
Jimmy Milne	1946–47	Harry Leyland	1967–68
Bob Pryde	1949–52	Alan Saunders	1968
Ted Goodier	1952–54	Ian McNeill	1968–70
Walter Crook	1954–55	Gordon Milne	1970–72
Ron Suart	1955–56	Les Rigby	1972–74
Billy Cooke	1956	Brian Tiler	1974–76
Sam Barkas	1957	Ian McNeill	1976–81
Trevor Hitchen	1957–58	Larry Lloyd	1981–83
Malcolm Barrass	1958–59	Harry McNally	1983–85
Jimmy Shirley	1959	Bryan Hamilton	1985–86
Pat Murphy	1959–60	Ray Mathias	1986–89
Allenby Chilton	1960	Bryan Hamilton	1989–93
Johnny Ball	1961–63	Dave Philpotts	1993
Allan Brown	1963–66	Kenny Swain	1993–94
		Graham Barrow	1994–95
		John Deehan	1995–

Manchester City

There is no doubt that Latics have a special relationship with Manchester City. It was a bond which proved a big help in pushing the club towards the goal everyone at Springfield Park was aiming for . . . entry into League football.

MANCHESTER CITY

VERSUS

WIGAN ATHLETIC

F.A. CHALLENGE CUP—3rd Round

SATURDAY

2nd JANUARY, 1971

Kick-off 3-15 p.m.

NEWS 1/- 5p

WE WANT MORE! ... this was the goal scored by Neil Young at Hull last season, our only goal in the F.A. Cup. Let's hope we can notch a few more this time! Picture: County Press

The programme for our match at Manchester City in the Third Round of the F. A. Cup on 2 January 1971.

Manchester City were Latics' guests on the occasion of the opening of the floodlights, when some 10,000 spectators watched the game.

The fixture with Manchester City at Maine Road in 1971 was a more serious affair. That season we were lucky to draw City at Maine Road in the 3rd Round of the F.A. Cup. With Gordon Milne as our player-manager, we delighted a crowd of 46,212 by the enormous fight we put up in losing the game by the only goal. It doesn't seem over twenty years ago that Joe Corrigan was flinging himself across his goal to fingertip a head from Geoff Davies out of the corner of the net just minutes after Colin Bell had scored what proved to be the winner!

It is certainly nice to have friends in high places and they didn't come any higher than Manchester City on 19 September 1977, when, as leaders of the First Division, they brought their star-studded line-up to Springfield Park for a friendly match.

The two clubs last met in the Second Round of the Milk Cup in 1982–83. The Latics gave their First Division opponents a severe testing in the 1st Leg and were unlucky not to clinch victory as City were at times forced to rely on an 11-man defence in a 1–1 draw at Springfield Park. It was certainly no disgrace to come away from Maine Road the losers by 2–0 and the performance of teenagers John Butler, David Lowe and Steve Walsh was a tremendous plus.

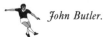

John Butler.

 David Lowe (above) and Steve Walsh (below).

May Day

On Saturday 1 May 1954, with the first team being kept back for a Lancashire Junior Cup Final replay with Horwich R.M.I., the Latics fulfilled *two* Lancashire Combination fixtures the same day—the reserves filling in against South Liverpool (h 2–2) and the third team going to Rossendale United and losing 4–1.

Harry McNally

Harry McNally never appeared in the Football League, spending most of his playing days with Skelmersdale United, where he was also a coach in his latter days there.

After managing Altrincham and Southport he joined Wigan Athletic as assistant manager and chief scout before taking over the managerial reins in July 1983. In his two seasons in charge the Latics struggled against relegation and in March 1985 he made way for Bryan Hamilton. Moving to Chester City he took the club to runners-up spot in Division Four in 1985–86 and to eighth in Division Three in 1988–89.

Despite losing their Sealand Road ground and a dramatic drop in attendances, McNally managed to keep Chester in the Third Division and was rewarded with a four-year contract. But after a poor start to the 1992–93 season he was sacked and replaced by Graham Barrow.

Ian McNeill

Ian McNeill was born in Glasgow and received his education in that soccer-mad city. Despite receiving offers from Everton and Wolves, he joined Aberdeen as a schoolboy in 1950 and during that period, played five times for the Scottish Youth International XI.

His part-time career with Aberdeen was interrupted by a spell of National Service in Kenya among the Mau Mau. His first team appearances were somewhat spasmodic, so Ian asked for and was granted a transfer. He joined Leicester City for a fee of £5,000 in 1956 and in his first season at Filbert Street, gained a Second Divisional medal as a member of the Leicester City side which gained promotion in 1956–57.

First Division life got off to an exciting start with Ian scoring a hat-trick against Sunderland in the second game. In 1959–60, he was transferred to Brighton and Hove Albion for that club's then record fee of £10,000. He spent four happy years at the Goldstone Ground before ending his full-time playing career with Southend United in 1965–66.

He first became player-coach to Ross County and later manager, during which time Ross County won the Highland League Championship for the first time in their history.

Ian McNeill then applied for and was appointed manager by ambitious Wigan Athletic for their first season in the Northern Premier League. They finished a very creditable second, yet in spite of promising performances in the F.A. Cup and the pre-Christmas league programme, things suddenly went sour at Springfield Park and after a brief laying bare of conflicting opinions in public, Ian McNeill was dismissed.

After spells with Salisbury Town and Ross County for a second term in which the Highland League side won the Scottish Qualifying Cup Final, McNeill burned his pride and in 1976 rejoined the Latics. It was however a different Wigan Athletic to the one which Ian McNeill had previously known. Money was very tight, interest in the Northern Premier League was on the wane and a miracle was needed to revitalise soccer in Wigan.

What followed is history, with Ian McNeill's team going from strength to strength. They gained F.A. Cup glory at Birmingham, second place in the Northern Premier League and of course entry into the Football League. At the centre of all that was Ian McNeill.

He left Wigan in 1981 to join Chelsea as assistant-manager, later becoming manager at Shrewsbury. Today, he is chief scout at neighbours Bolton Wanderers.

Ian McNeill often held his ground, at times when it would have been easier to give way. Wigan Athletic Football Club has been very fortunate to twice have the privilege of the canny Scot's undoubted managerial expertise.

Mercantile Centenary Festival

The Mercantile Centenary Festival took place at Wembley over the weekend of 16–17 April 1988, though both of Wigan's games were played on the Saturday.

Qualification for the tournament was based on the number of League points won in the first 15 league games after 1 November 1987. Eight clubs came from Division One, four from Division Two and two each from the Third and Fourth Divisions.

Latics' 15 games after 1 November brought 10 wins, 3 draws and 2 defeats. We finished 'second' in the Third Division table behind Sunderland. One of our defeats came in the 'last' game away at Chester and if Blackpool hadn't beaten Notts County, the team from Meadow Lane would have pipped us at the post.

The official attendance for day one of the festival was 43,000. Playing twenty minutes each way, Wigan and Sunderland fought out a goalless draw, before Latics won 2–1 on penalties, scored by Stan McEwan and Paul Cook. In the quarter-finals, Chris Thompson

 Latics and Sunderland take the field at Wembley before the match we won on penalties.

scored Latics' goal in a 1–1 draw with Sheffield Wednesday, though this time, we lost 2–3 in the penalty shoot-out with Bobby Campbell missing his attempt.

Sheffield Wednesday eventually lost in the final to Notts Forest (3–2 on penalties) after beating Manchester United (2–1) in the semi-finals.

Colin Methven

Since Colin Methven made his full League début for Wigan Athletic against Doncaster Rovers in the Fourth Division game at Belle Vue in October 1979, the rugged Scot's performances quite rightly earned him the title of 'Mr Consistency'.

Former holder of the Latics' record for the most first team appearances with 296, one of the most interesting things about him is that he never missed a game at a competitive level through injury. You could count the number of poor games he had on one hand. If ever £30,000 constituted a bargain, then the fee paid to East Fife for Methven was surely the case.

Superb in the air, solid on the ground, Colin was also handy for a few goals.

Yet he never had any ambition to be a professional footballer, merely to play as much as possible and it was only when East Fife converted his professional contract into a proper contract, at the age of nineteen, he suddenly thought that perhaps he had a chance of making a career in football.

As captain of the Wigan Athletic side, he became a firm favourite with the fans at Springfield Park who elected him Player of the Year in 1979–80 and 1984–85. But perhaps his greatest honour was in 1981–82 when his fellow professionals voted him into the Fourth Division Select XI.

Gordon Milne

Gordon Milne was a half-back and began his career with Preston North End in 1958. He then moved on to Liverpool and played in that magnificent side of the mid-sixties. While he was at Liverpool, he gained two League Championship medals, an F.A. Cup Winner's Medal and fourteen England caps. On leaving Anfield, he joined Blackpool for £30,000 and it was from there that he joined the Latics to take up his first managerial post early in 1970. He followed in his father's footsteps, for Jimmy Milne was boss at Springfield Park for a short time when Latics were in the Cheshire League just after the war.

Although he guided Wigan to the runners-up spot in his first season as manager of the Northern Premier League side, it is for his exploits as player-manager in the famous 1970–71 season that he will be remembered by Latics fans. He steered Latics to the Third Round of the F.A. Cup beating Peterborough United along the way, before Latics were finally put out by First Division Manchester City at Maine Road, after a performance that was rated one of the best by a Wigan team while a non-league side. At the end of the season, the Northern Premier League title came to Springfield Park, and the following year, Third Division Halifax Town were knocked out of the F.A. Cup by Latics.

Gordon Milne's exploits did not go unnoticed and while he was at Wigan, he was appointed manager-coach of the England Youth Team.

It was obvious that the popular, thoughtful manager would move on to bigger things, so it came as no surprise, when in 1972, it was announced that Gordon Milne would be joining First Division Coventry City.

Most Matches

In years gone by it was quite commonplace to see Latics involved in more than 70 first team games in a season.

By today's terms that seems ludicrous, but no doubt the directors of that time considered the winning of several trophies each season as ample justification of the heavy fixture list.

One such season was 1966–67 when the Latics, then members of the Cheshire County League played a staggering 86 first team matches—a club record that will never be beaten. However, the reward for all the hard work was the winning of five trophies—The Northern Floodlight League and Knockout Cup, the Liverpool Non-League Cup, the Lancashire F.A. Floodlight Cup and the Case Trophy for the Cheshire League runners-up.

Neutral Grounds

After battling their way into the first round proper of the 1969–70 F.A. Cup competition, Latics drew Port Vale at Springfield Park. There followed two epic struggles, the Vale holding Latics to a 1–1 scoreline then Latics holding Port Vale at Vale Park 2–2. The second replay was held at Old Trafford and the spectators saw a game fit for such a great stadium. Latics forced Vale into extra-time but lost a goal in the last minute.

The Latics had a fantastic run in the F.A. Challenge Trophy of 1972–73 that earned them a place in the final.

The fourth round saw 300 minutes of football as Morecambe fought out a goalless draw at Springfield Park and then drew 1–1 at Morecambe, before conceding the only goal of the second replay at Ewood Park. The semi-final against Stafford Rangers played at Vale Park was goalless, but in the replayed at Oldham's Boundary Park, Oates scored the only goal of the game to put Wigan in the final.

Boundary Park was also the venue of the 1988–89 Lancashire Manx Group Match between Latics and Bolton Wanderers. A new venue was needed after Springfield Borough R.L.F.C. had been sharing the Latics' ground making it unfit and Bolton had refused to stage the tie at Burnden Park.

The Latics have also played in numerous finals on a neutral ground:

Competition	Season	Opponents	Venue	Score
Lancs Junior Cup	1934–35	Fleetwood	Deepdale	2–3
Lancs Junior Cup	1938–39	South Liverpool	Anfield	0–3
Lancs Junior Cup	1951–52	Lancaster City	Deepdale	2–2
Lancs Junior Cup	1951–52	Lancaster City	Bloomfield Road	1–2
Lancs Junior Cup	1952–53	Lancaster City	Ewood Park	1–1
Lancs Junior Cup	1952–53	Lancaster City	Ewood Park	2–1
Lancs Junior Cup	1953–54	Horwich R.M.I.	Ewood Park	2–2
Lancs Junior Cup	1953–54	Horwich R.M.I.	Chorley	2–1
Liverpool Non-League	1957–58	New Brighton	Anfield	3–3
Lancs Junior Cup	1958–59	Chorley	Ewood Park	1–4
Lancs Junior Cup	1961–62	Morecambe	Deepdale	1–3
Liverpool Non-League	1961–62	New Brighton	Anfield	0–2
Lancs Junior Cup	1964–65	Chorley	Deepdale	1–4
Lancs Junior Cup	1965–66	Netherfield	Morecambe	2–0
Liverpool Non-League	1965–66	South Liverpool	Southport	2–0 aet
Lancs Junior Cup	1967–68	Marine	Deepdale	2–0
Lancs Challenge Trophy	1969–70	Skelmersdale	Chorley	1–2
Lancs Challenge Trophy	1971–72	Netherfield	Chorley	3–1

Newcastle United

Of all the cup ties played by Wigan Athletic, the match against Newcastle United at St James' Park in the Third Round of the F.A. Cup on 9 January 1954 was probably the most remarkable.

There were the minnows from the Lancashire Combination facing a star-studded and glittering First Division team at the height of its football prowess.

Newcastle's team sheet was filled with names that became legends— Simpson, Batty, McMichael, Scouler, Brennan, Stokoe, Walker,

Bert Lomas saves as the Magpies attack in the F. A. Cup Third Round replay at Springfield Park.

Broadis, Monkhouse, Milburn and Mitchell, whilst Latics fielded a team of relative unknowns—Lomas, Lindsay, Parkinson, Lynn, Mycock, Banks, Butler, Livesey, Lomax, Lyon and Hindle.

The attendance that day of 52,222 made it the largest crowd to watch a game involving Wigan Athletic.

It was a slip by Mycock that led to Newcastle taking the lead. Off balance he kicked a clearance which sailed to the ever dangerous Broadis who made no mistake in putting the Magpies one up. This gave the home side more confidence, but the Latics held out to go in at half-time just the one goal down.

The second half began differently and within seven minutes of the re-start, Latics were even through a Jack Lyon goal. In the 75th minute, the unbelievable happened as Livesey cracked home Hindle's pass to put Latics 2–1 up. While the Wigan supporters were still shaking hands on the terraces, Jackie Milburn launched himself from the kick-off on a death or glory run which resulted in a brilliant solo goal to level things up. The remaining 13 minutes saw Lomax pull off a brilliant save from a Milburn volley, while Latics' Tommy Hindle had a goal disallowed for offside. The full-time whistle went with the

scores standing at 2–2. Following this incredible result, the Latics were in a confident mood for the return fixture at Springfield Park. The match however got off to an unsporting start when Stan Seymour the Newcastle chairman refused to let the team change in Wigan's make-shift dressing rooms, calling the facilities 'crude'. His remark was very insensitive given that Latics supporters and directors had worked hard in their attempts to repair the damage caused by the great fire.

Wigan fielded the same side whilst the Magpies made several changes. The atmosphere was electric amongst the capacity 25,000 fans with more either standing outside or hanging out of the windows of the houses overlooking the ground.

Newcastle were the first to draw blood, taking the lead in the 13th minute when Keeble headed home Mitchell's inch perfect cross. The Magpies extended their lead in the 34th minute when White controlled a loose ball in a goalmouth scramble to fire home. Undeterred, the Latics quickly pulled a goal back when centre-forward Lomax smacked a left foot shot past Simpson's outstretched arms.

Within minutes of the second half, controversy flared. Lyon lobbed a thoughtful one at Simpson, who caught the ball while stepping back and in doing so the ball appeared to cross the line. The crowd as one man shouted 'goal!'

It was not to be as the referee ruled against Wigan's claims and ordered play to continue. The decision seemed to upset Latics momentum and despite holding on till the 71st minute, they eventually succumbed to a Broadis header to put the visitors 3–1 up.

Nine minutes from time, Lomax pulled a goal back for Latics, but it was only to be a consolation goal. In fact, Newcastle were so much in control that they could have made it 4–2 had Mitchell not stabbed an easy chance wide.

Thus the Latics went out of the Cup, but in fine style and they had certainly given the League giants a nasty scare.

Newport County

Newport County played more matches than any other ex-member of the Football League, after joining the newly formed Third Division in 1920.

'The Ironsides' as Newport were known, became regular opponents of ours throughout our early seasons in the Football League. During our Fourth Division days, we met on four occasions and lost on every one! They won promotion from the Fourth Division at the end of the 1979–80 season, so the next time we met was in the Third Division in 1982–83, when County again won both fixtures. In fact, it wasn't until our eighth encounter that we secured the points when David Lowe scored the only goal of the game in front of 2,903 spectators at Springfield Park.

Newport's last visit to us was in 1986–87 when they won 2–1. In 1988 they were relegated to the Vauxhall Conference and were disbanded during the following season.

 David Lowe bursts clear of the Newport County defence.

Northern Premier League

The Northern Premier League was formed for two basic reasons. Firstly, it was decided by a collection of clubs that the north needed a 'super league' for non-League teams in the area who were too strong for their respective leagues. And secondly, after many disappointed trips to the F.A. Headquarters, non-League clubs realised that there would be a greater chance of League status if the contenders came from a proven competition. Wigan Athletic were amongst the founder members of this group of clubs and in 1968–69 competed in the opening season of the Northern Premier League.

Under new manager Ian McNeill, the Latics got off to a winning start 2–0 away to Scarborough with goals from Billy Sutherland and Alan Ryan. It was a good omen for the future, for that season Wigan finished as runners-up to Macclesfield Town. The 1969–70 season once again saw a two-horse race between Wigan and Macclesfield with the Silkmen once again snatching the title. But it was a close run race all depending on the last match. Macclesfield visited South Shields; if the home side had won by three clear goals, then the league title would have gone to Wigan. Macclesfield held on to the title however, going down 3–1 to pip the Latics with a goal average of 1·756 compared to Wigan's 1·750.

During the following season, the match on Boxing Day against league leaders Stafford Rangers attracted 8,107 spectators, a number which still stands as a Northern Premier League record. Latics won 4–1 with goals from Milne, Fleming (penalty), Oates and Davies. Having beaten the halfway leaders, it was inevitable that Athletic would go on to win the Premier League title at their third attempt.

For the next two seasons, the club finished third in the league. In 1973–74 they finished second and then in the following season went on to take the title for a second time, gaining a record number of points in doing so (72). The final match of that season was against Scarborough and Latics revenged themselves of their Wembley defeat two years earlier, beating them 2–0 to clinch the league title. For the record that season's record was:

P	W	D	L	F	A	Pts
46	33	6	7	94	38	72

The 1975–76 and 1976–77 seasons were not happy ones for the club. In the first, Wigan could only manage to finish 6th in the league, the first time they had ever finished outside the top three in the history of the Northern Premier League. The following season saw the results on the field grow more and more disappointing, the club languishing at the foot of the table. Arthur Horrocks returned as club chairman and a new optimism filled the club, the team spirit returned and results began to pick up, the team finishing 14th that season.

Following the signing of the popular Maurice Whittle on a free transfer from Oldham Athletic, the Latics grew in confidence—a confidence that was reflected in an unbeaten run which stretched from October 1977 to January 1978.

A decision was reached by the Northern Premier League—the club finishing second would get a crack at applying for the League. As the season drew to its climax, Boston United whose lead at the top looked unassailable were told that their ground was not up to the required standard. The battle was between three clubs; Bangor City, Scarborough and Latics. The final matches of the season arrived and still the second place was undecided. The Latics were at home to Bangor City and had to win to put Scarborough out of contention. Five minutes from the end they were 1–0 down, but late goals from Corrigan and Wilkie made it 2–1. Wigan were, however, still uncertain of the runners-up spot, it all depended on their last game of the season at Matlock. Peter Houghton scored the only goal in what was to be the club's last Northern Premier League match.

Latics' full record in the Northern Premier League is:

P	W	D	L	F	A	Pts
438	236	120	82	763	404	592

Olympic Games

Formers Latics 'keeper *Harry Sharratt* who was capped for England whilst playing with Bishop Auckland was chosen for the Great Britain Olympic Games team in Melbourne 1956.

Opening Day of the Season

In the sixteen seasons since Latics were admitted to the Football League they have only won once on the opening day of the season. That was thanks to the only goal of the game, scored by Graham Barrow as Wigan beat Swansea City at the Vetch Field in 1985–86.

They have, however, drawn six of the remaining fixtures, including an eight-goal thriller at Notts County in 1987–88.

One would have to go a long way to see a more entertaining first match of the season than Latics' visit to Lytham in the 1960–61 Lancashire Combination fixture. The game was a thriller, won 6–5 by Latics, who despite being a goal down in 20 seconds, led 3–1 after only six minutes!

Own Goals

Perhaps the strangest own-goal came at Burnden Park on 21 September 1991, when recently returned Latics midfielder *Tony Kelly* then in Bolton colours, lobbed Wanderers' on-loan goalkeeper Andy Dibble from fully 20 yards when under no pressure whatsoever. This was ironic in that apart from being a former Wigan player at the time, it was his first goal in a Bolton shirt!

Harry Parkinson

Probably one of the most popular players ever to turn out in Latics colours was left-back Harry Parkinson.

A local lad through and through, Harry played for Chorley Schoolboys before serving in the army during the war years. He returned to sign for Wigan Athletic in 1946, claiming it to be the proudest day of his life.

Harry played ten seasons as a full-back for Latics and today still holds the club record for consecutive appearances in the first team—a staggering 212. Harry only ever played for Wigan and when he finally hung up his boots, he took over as Youth Team coach, a post he held for twelve years until he finally called it a day in 1974.

A technician with a Wigan dentist, Harry was also churchwarden at Standish Parish Church and chairman of the Wrightington Hospital League of Friends.

However, Wigan fans will remember Harry Parkinson as the tigerish full-back of a very successful era, when he played in the same team as Kenny Banks, Billy Lomax and Dave Mycock. Many fans still regard that 1953–54 side as the finest team ever to grace Springfield Park.

Penalties

On Wednesday 25 September 1963, Wigan goalkeeper *Jeff MacKay* had to face four spot kicks just before half-time in a Cheshire County League game at Winsford United. He saved the first three but was adjudged to have moved and was finally beaten by the fourth. This remarkable penalty incident was probably unique in the annals of the league. The game ended in a 2–2 draw.

When Latics visited Moss Rose on 24 October 1970 in a Northern Premier League fixture, Macclesfield who had won the League for the first two seasons of its existence, were on top of the League. That day, Latics won 3–1 to inflict upon the Silkmen only their third defeat in

46 home Premier League games. In the last minute, the Macclesfield scorer Fidler, fluffed a penalty—TWICE!

Later that season, Peterborough United visited Springfield Park in the F.A. Cup 2nd Round. At 1–1, it looked set for a replay until Oates chased a ball to the bye-line before clipping it into the penalty area and against the outstretched hand of Peterborough's left-half Wright. Jim Fleming stepped up coolly to send the 'keeper the wrong way from the spot kick and Latics went through to the 3rd Round for the first time in seventeen years. The following season, the club were dismissed by Barnet from the F.A. Challenge Trophy at Springfield Park by 2–1. Both Joe Fletcher and Jim Fleming missing penalties, although Fletcher did score one!

In 1987–88, five different Latics players all missed penalties. Alex Cribley had scored all three he had taken, but was injured—the shamed players were: Barry Knowles (Grimsby Town [a] 2–0), Paul Jewell (Aldershot [h] 4–0), Paul Cook (Rotherham United [a] 1–1), Stan McEwan (Grimsby Town [h] 0–1) and Bobby Campbell (in the penalty shoot-out at Wembley *v.* Sheffield Wednesday 2–3).

Among the best goalkeeping performances against penalties in the Football League was that achieved by Phil Hughes. He saved three out of the four penalties he faced in the 1989–90 season—Bury (h 0–0), Bolton Wanderers (h 2–0), Bristol City (h 2–3)—the one that got away was also in the Bristol City game. That same season, Nigel Adkins

 *Alex Cribley.*

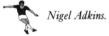
Nigel Adkins.

saved a penalty at Anfield, though Liverpool won 5–2, but conceded one at Burnden Park as Wigan went down 3–2.

Bryan Griffiths is the top Latics penalty-taker in League football. In all competitions, he has missed three—*v.* Chester City in the Leyland DAF Cup on 6 November 1990, his kick was initially saved by ex-Latics player Billy Stewart, but Bryan followed up to put in the rebound, the first goal in a 4–0 win, but technically a penalty miss. The next came in the 4–1 Lancashire Manx Cup Final win against Preston North End on 13 August 1991. His last miss from the spot was in the 1991–92 season in the Latics 2–0 win over Mansfield Town—it would have given him a hat-trick!

More recently, the Latics surrendered the Marsden Cup in the cruellest of ways with Spaniards Isidro Diaz and Roberto Martinez the villains of the moment as Wigan lost 4–2 to Blackpool in a penalty shoot-out.

Plastic

There have been four Football League clubs that have replaced their normal grass playing pitches with artificial surfaces at one stage or another.

Queen's Park Rangers were the first in 1981, but the Loftus Road plastic was discarded in 1988 in favour of a return to turf without the Latics playing on it. Luton Town (1985), Oldham Athletic (1986) and Preston North End (1986) followed. We never played on the Boundary Park surface and on our only visit to Kenilworth Road, home of Luton Town, we lost 4–2 in the 2nd Round (2nd Leg) of the 1987–88 League Cup.

We have, however, been regular visitors to Deepdale and though our record on their plastic pitch is not a good one, it is probably no worse than those of most clubs.

At Deepdale

Season	Competition	Score	Season	Competition	Score
1987–88	Division 3	1–0	1989–90	Leyland DAF	2–1
1988–89	Division 3	2–2	1990–91	Division 3	1–2
1988–89	League Cup	0–1	1991–92	Division 3	0–3
1989–90	Division 3	1–1	1992–93	Division 3	0–2

Player of the Year

This award by Wigan supporters dates from season 1968–69 and the winners have been as follows:

1968–69	Ian Gillibrand	1982–83	John Butler
1969–70	Dennis Reeves	1983–84	Tony Kelly
1970–71	Ian Gillibrand	1984–85	Colin Methven
1971–72	Billy Sutherland	1985–86	Barry Knowles
1972–73	Graham Oates	1986–87	David Hamilton
1973–74	Albert Jackson	1987–88	David Thompson
1974–75	Fred Molyneux	1988–89	David Thompson

1975–76	Not Awarded	1989–90	Peter Atherton
1976–77	Micky Worswick	1990–91	Peter Atherton
1977–78	Tommy Gore	1991–92	Phil Daley
1978–79	John Brown	1992–93	Allen Tankard
1979–80	Colin Methven	1993–94	Andy Lyons
1980–81	Les Bradd	1994–95	Neill Rimmer
1981–82	Jimmy Weston		

Young Player of the Year

The winners have been:

1984–85	Warren Aspinall	1990–91	Alan Johnson
1985–86	Warren Aspinall	1991–92	Phil Jones
1986–87	Paul Beesley	1992–93	John Robertson
1987–88	Paul Cook	1993–94	Matthew Carrager
1988–89	Peter Atherton	1994–95	Matthew Carrager
1989–90	Alan Johnson		

David Thompson.

Play-Offs

The play-offs were introduced in 1986–87 to settle the promotion and relegation issues between Divisions and to assist in the reduction of the First Division from twenty-two to twenty over two seasons.

The Latics were involved in the 1987 play-offs after finishing in fourth position in Division Three. They were paired against Swindon Town in the semi-finals. After leading 2–0 inside the first 15 minutes with goals from Chris Thompson and David Lowe, suicidal defending allowed Swindon to score three goals in the last 18 minutes. In the return leg, luckless Latics hit the woodwork, but not the net and went out after a goalless draw.

Points

Under the three points for a win system, which was introduced in 1981–82, the Latics' best points tally was the 91 points in that season, which saw us gain promotion. Our best points haul under the old two points for a win system was 55 which we achieved in our first two seasons in the Football League.

At non-League level, our best tally was 72 which we achieved in 1965–66 (Lancashire Combination) and 1974–75 (Northern Premier League). Our worst record under either system was the meagre 25 points secured in 1946–47.

Port Vale

The first match ever played at Springfield Park by Wigan Athletic took place on 27 August 1932, when, about a year after Wigan Borough had folded, a team under the managership of former international centre-half Charlie Spencer took the field against Port Vale Reserves.

Port Vale Reserves were considered to be the best side in the Cheshire League at that time and against such strong opposition Athletic, who a week previously had no team at all, signed on, put up a performance that did the side every credit, though sadly they went down 2–0.

Port Vale also provided the opposition for the first match of Latics' Easter programme during their first season in the Football League— the first time a Wigan player scored a hat-trick since we were admitted to the League.

With only thirty minutes to go, the Latics were three goals down. Ian McNeill then played his master stroke. He substituted skipper Noel Ward and sent on striker Derek Brownbill in an attempt to rescue what was surely a lost cause.

Surprisingly enough, gaps began to appear in the Vale defence and when Peter Houghton pulled a goal back, muted cheers greeted what looked like a consolation goal. A minute later the cheers increased as Houghton scored his second goal. Sure enough Peter Houghton completed his hat-trick and all the disappointments of the first hour were forgotten as the crowd of 8,452 urged the Latics on.

Springfield Park erupted when substitute Derek Brownbill hooked in Latics' fourth goal and the match was all over when Mick Moore scored a fifth to crown what surely must rank as one of the greatest games ever seen at Springfield Park.

Programme of the Year

In 1993–94, Wigan Athletic won the Commercial Managers' Association Third Division Programme of the Year Award. This was sponsored by Citizen Watches and termed the Citizen Watch Programme of the Year. Though there are many Programme of the Year awards issued by the different organisations, this is the most prestigious.

In 1981–82, the Latics programme which won them a cup for the best programme in the Fourth Division was in the words of the judges, 'Way above anything else produced in the Division.'

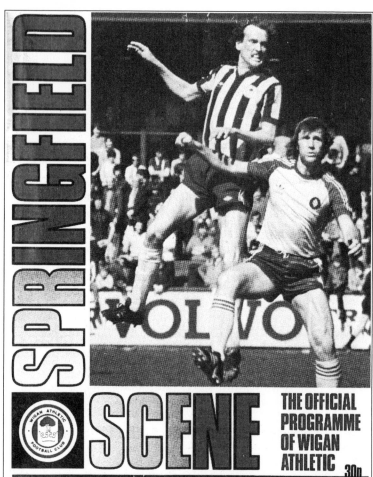

Front cover of the Latics programme for the 1981–82 season.

Promotion

The Latics have won promotion in the Football League on just one occasion—so far!

It was in 1981–82 that we finished third in the Fourth Division behind Bradford City and Sheffield United. Eamonn O'Keefe arrived from Everton for a record £65,000 and Second Division Chelsea were sent packing in the League Cup before League champions Aston Villa ended the run, snatching victory three minutes from time.

Our twin strikers Les Bradd (19) and Peter Houghton (15) scored 34 of our 80 League goals and at Scunthorpe, we won 7–2 to record our biggest away win in the Football League.

Our analysis was:

	Home					Away					
P	W	D	L	F	A	W	D	L	F	A	Pts
46	17	5	1	47	18	9	8	6	33	28	91

Sir Alf Ramsey

The most famous of English managers, Sir Alf Ramsey, was in charge of Birmingham City whom the Latics visited in the Third Round of the F.A. Cup in 1977–78 in what was arguably the most important game ever played in the history of the club.

Though Latics lost 4–0, they won a place in the League, for on that day, their style of football, the behaviour of the fans and the gentlemanly presence of the club's officials gained the admiration and support of the First Division opposition.

Though beaten, Wigan left the field to tumultuous applause. Their football attracted the attention of Sir Alf Ramsey, who visited the dressing room after the match to congratulate the team.

Rapid Scoring

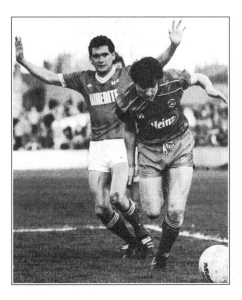

Latics have scored many goals in the opening minute of a game of which Paul Jewell's in the match against Rotherham United on 31 October 1987 is one of the most recent.

Our best effort in the Football League at rapid scoring was five goals in 19 minutes, defeating Port Vale (5–3) at home on Good Friday 1979, after being three goals down!

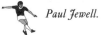

Paul Jewell.

Relegation

Up until the 1992–93 season, the Latics had never suffered the ignominy of relegation, but after just one season in the Second Division that record disappeared.

Prior to that season, Latics lowest position in the Football League was 18th which they achieved in seasons 1982–83 and 1989–90, both in Division Three. Last season the Latics ended the campaign in 19th position. Yet in 1946–47, the club finished bottom of the Cheshire League with just 25 points from the 42 matches played.

Robin Park

It now looks as if the club's move to Robin Park will be going ahead, with the Latics aiming to be in their new home for the start of the 1997–98 season. The playing surface will be contained within a running track and will have stands on two sides only, the ends being left empty. The initial capacity will be in the region of 12,000 (all seated). Should the Latics reach Division One and the club's attendances warrant an increase, the council have promised to build over the track and complete the stadium by building new stands behind the goals.

Rugby League

Jack Arkwright the Latics' goalkeeper in 1957–58, who only missed one cup game, later went on to play Rugby League for St Helens.

One of Wigan's best signings came in November 1980 from the famous local Rugby League club. No, they didn't get themselves a flying winger, the man in question was groundsman, *Billy Mitchell*. He was at Central Park for many years and made immediate improvements to the playing surface of Springfield Park.

In 1987–88, Springfield Park also became a venue of Rugby League with Springfield Borough sharing the ground with Latics—it was an unwise move.

Scottish League

In 1972, the Latics created a minor sensation in the world of football by applying for admission to the Scottish League. This did the club no good at all, as for the next three years Wigan were completely ignored at the A.G.M. of the Football League.

Second Division

Our only season in the Second Division ended recently with relegation to the Third. Our first game in this Division ended in a 2–1 defeat at the hands of Stockport County, whilst our first points came with an excellent 3–2 win at Millmoor against Rotherham United. Our last game in the Division saw us draw 0–0 at Bournemouth on 8 May 1993.

Our playing record in Division Two is as follows:

P	W	D	L	F	A
46	10	11	25	43	72

Select Band

Warren Aspinall is the only Latics player to notch over 20 Football League goals in a season, scoring 21 in 1985–86.

At non-League level, there have been six occasions when a player has scored more than 40 league goals—Harry Lyon achieving this feat on two occasions. All were in the Cheshire League and were:

Jack Roberts	46 in 1934–35
John Wallbanks	40 in 1936–37
Horace Thomas	40 in 1938–39
Harry Lyon	45 in 1964–65
Bert Llewellyn	49 in 1965–66
Harry Lyon	42 in 1965–66

Charlie Spencer

The first manager Latics ever had, was ex-Newcastle United captain and England International, Charlie Spencer.

Charlie's first managerial appointment had been with a moderately successful Tunbridge Wells side.

When he was appointed player-manager in August 1932, Charlie Spencer had just a few weeks to get a team together. After some frantic efforts and shrewd persuasion, he managed to bring a side together, and it proved to be one of the best-ever to wear the colours of Wigan Athletic. By the opening date of the season the team had been welded into some form of playing unit, but in front of 5,106 spectators they went down 2–0 to Port Vale Reserves.

By the following Wednesday, Spencer had whipped his virgin team into shape and they beat Tranmere Rovers Reserves 5–1.

The famous forward line of Armes, Robson, Roberts, Felton and Scott is rated by many to be the best Wigan Athletic forward line of all time. All the players were signed by Charlie Spencer in time for the 1933–34 season. The team in which this forward line starred made footballing history. In the 1933–34 season, Latics were drawn away at Carlisle in the F.A. Cup. Carlisle were then in the Third Division North of the Football League and the Latics in the Cheshire League. That didn't seem to matter because the result staggered football— Carlisle United 1 Wigan Athletic 6—a score that still stands as a record for a non-League club playing away against a Football League side in a cup-tie.

Charlie Spencer was more than just a good manager, he was a very strict disciplinarian and a great character.

One of the best known stories about him concerns the ritual which surrounded his arrival at the ground in the morning. At the time, he lived in Blackpool and was one of the few people in the area to have a car. The players, all full-time professionals had been told to report every morning at 10.00 a.m. and Charlie Spencer generally arrived ten minutes later. The players used to lounge around the dressing rooms until they heard the familiar sound of their manager's car drawing up outside. That was the signal to move, for by the time that Charlie

walked into the dressing room, the players were changed into their kit and ready for training!

By the time he left Wigan for First Division Grimsby Town, Athletic had won practically every honour open to a non-League side at that time. On his departure, he promised Latics he would bring his new team to play them in a friendly. It was a promise he was to keep, for more than six years later, he brought his star-studded side to Springfield Park after the end of the war and they beat Latics 5–2 in front of a crowd of 16,000, still a record for a friendly match at Springfield Park.

After managing Grimsby Town, he joined York City. In fact, in the early fifties he applied for the managerial vacancy when Latics appointed another great character, Ted Goodier.

Dogged by ill-health for some years, he died in Blackpool at the age of fifty-four where he had spent most of his life. Charlie Spencer is still held in awe and great respect by those who supported the club in its early days.

Sponsors

In February 1995, David Whelan, the former Blackburn Rovers full-back and club sponsor through one of his companies (JJB Sports), bought the club from Stephen Gage and Nick Bitel.

Springfield Park

Springfield Park first came into existence during the reign of Queen Victoria, but it wasn't until the formation of Wigan County in 1897 that the ground first came to be used as a venue for Association Football.

Prior to that historic introduction, Springfield Park had been used as a sports arena, boasting a concrete bicycle track, a half-mile running

track and some fine sporting equipment used especially in Victorian times.

The first professional match to be staged at Springfield Park took place on 1 September 1897 when Wigan County played Burton Swifts in a friendly match.

The next club to use Springfield Park was named Wigan Town. They were forced to share the ground with Wigan R.L.F.C. After Town folded in 1904, it was another fifteen years or so before anyone had the courage to start again. Wigan Borough lasted until 12 league games into the 1931–32 season when due to financial difficulties the club went into voluntary liquidation.

After prolonged negotiations, Wigan Athletic purchased Springfield Park for the princely sum of £2,800 from the owners of Woodhouse Lane dog track. There was one very interesting clause in the agreement of sale which read that the new owners must guarantee Springfield Park would never be used for greyhound racing!

This valuable acquisition consisted of 14 acres of land, a wooden stand with seating for 2,000 spectators and shelter on the popular side. Though the ground was kept in reasonably good order throughout the

 Springfield Park.

war by the older directors, the old wooden stand needed major repairs and the popular side shelter re-roofing.

During the 1952–53 season, Latics' main stand was razed to the ground by fire and despite some enthusiastic fund-raising by the club's supporters, it took nearly a year to raise sufficient money to build a replacement. The flames not only engulfed the spectators facilities, but also the dressing rooms and baths.

The following season saw a record crowd of 27,526 watch Latics beat Hereford United 4–1—that record still stands today as the largest attendance ever recorded for a game between two non-League clubs excluding Wembley finals. However, the largest attendance recorded at Springfield Park is 30,611 when Wigan Borough entertained Shef-field Wednesday in 1929.

To assist the club financially, local builder and chairman, Lesley Jackson bought around four hundred acres of land from the club and built houses thereon. In the late 1950s this was an honourable move; however, with the Taylor Report and safety regulations today, the idea prohibits access around the complete area of the ground.

In October 1966, Manchester City officially opened the new £15,000 floodlights before a gate of 10,119.

It is interesting to note that in 1972, the club applied to build a greyhound track at the Park in an attempt to alleviate financial prob-lems. The idea was rejected however and the original condition re-mained in the early bill of sale for Springfield.

Once we were elected to the Football League, ground improve-ments had to be carried out by staff and numerous volunteers, to whom the club will be forever grateful.

Stirling Albion

Having really outgrown the Lancashire Combination, the club found themselves turning to almost gimmick matches to break the relative monotony.

One that comes to mind was a friendly game at Stirling Albion in Scotland, when the club chartered a plane to fly there. The heading in the local press was 'Latics take to the skies'.

There was nothing really remarkable about the match which ended in a 5–1 defeat for the Latics, but the story of the return home became a saga when on the club's return there was an announcement at Renfrew Airport that their plane had broken down. The party was forced to hitch home on separate flights as they became available.

Substitutes

Latics' first substitute in the Football League was Alan Crompton, who came on for Neil Davids in the second half of our third game of our first season, against Reading (a 0–2) but we had to wait until the visit of Port Vale later in the season for our first goalscoring number 12—Derek Brownbill, who scored the fourth goal in Latics' remarkable 5–3 win over Port Vale on Good Friday 1979.

The greatest number of substitutes used in a single season by the Latics under the single substitute rule was 36 in 1984–85, but since 1986–87 two substitutes have been allowed and in 1989–90 we used 76 in the 46 Division Three matches.

The greatest number of substitute appearances for the Latics has been made by Jimmy Carberry who had come on during 35 League games by the end of the 1991–92 season.

The highest number of substitute appearances in a season is 17 by Darren Patterson and Jimmy Carberry in the 1989–90 season. It was during that season that our earliest substitute appears to have come on. Against Walsall at home on 21 October 1989, Scott McGarvey who was on loan from Oldham Athletic at the time, went off injured after four minutes, to be replaced by Jimmy Carberry. In the same season, at home to Preston on 24 April 1990, Jimmy Carberry came on as substitute only to be taken off ten minutes later for the other substitute, Darren Patterson. This proved to be a very unpopular decision as many Latics fans protested towards the end of the game.

Our first substitute in non-League football was Allan Brown who came on during the 1966–67 season, the first season in non-League football in which substitutes were allowed.

Stuart Houghton was Latics' first substitute to score a goal in a non-League game when he came on for Bert Llewellyn in the Lancashire

Jimmy Carberry, seen here turning to celebrate a late goal scored against Crewe Alexandra.

Floodlit Cup 1st Round 2nd Leg game against Ashton United on Wednesday 1 February 1967. In fact, Stuart scored twice as Latics won this home leg 9–1 to win 10–3 on aggregate. Latics had fielded their reserve side in the 1st leg and had received a stern warning from the Lancashire Football Association.

Suspensions

The longest ever suspension served by a Latics player is that of Tony McLoughlin who was suspended for three months having been caught playing Sunday League football for an amateur side. He missed 21 games, including nine cup-ties.

However, on his return, he more than made up for lost time, scoring 7 goals in Latics' 11–1 Lancashire Floodlit Cup win over Darwen. Only 742 fans witnessed McLoughlin's scoring feat (14, 17, 24, 54, 59, 65, 90). It was a pity he couldn't have played in the previous game which saw Latics knocked out of the F.A. Trophy 1–0 by the eventual

Wembley finalists Telford United for whom Ron Flowers (Wolves and England) was player-manager in a game Latics dominated but couldn't score.

Television

The first Latics match to receive coverage on television was the Manchester City—Latics Third Round F.A. Cup-tie on 2 January 1971, recorded highlights of which were broadcast on the BBC's 'Match of the Day'.

On 20 September 1980, a goal in each half was enough to give Wigan victory 2–1 *v.* Bury in front of Granada's television cameras as well as the Fourth Division's biggest crowd. Wigan later slammed Granada TV for comments made by presenter Elton Welsby about having to televise Fourth Division games and about the quality of the performance.

Latics were also featured on 'Match of the Day' when clinching promotion to the Third Division and also on 'Grandstand' for the F.A. Cup Third Round replay on 8 January 1991. The cameras at that game proved that a perfectly good Don Page goal had been wrongly ruled out.

The one and only time the Latics have featured 'live' on television was when Tranmere Rovers knocked us out of the Northern Area semi-final of the Leyland DAF Cup 3–0 at Springfield Park—BsB covering that game.

Third Division

The Latics gained promotion to the Third Division at the end of the 1981–82 season, finishing third behind Bradford City and Sheffield United.

Our first game in the Third Division saw us go down 2–1 at Lincoln City with Les Bradd scoring our goal.

After three seasons of moderate placings, the Latics finished fourth in two consecutive campaigns (1985–86 and 1986–87). In the first season they missed promotion by one point, whilst the following season saw them miss out against Swindon Town in the play-offs. Our last game in the 'old' Division Three was on 2 May 1992 when we lost 3–2 at Reading.

Latics playing record in Division Three is as follows:

P	W	D	L	F	A
544	201	145	198	736	722

Three Amigos!

The Latics created quite a stir by signing three very highly rated Spaniards: Jesus Seba (a Spanish Under-21 international from Real Zaragoza, the European Cup Winners' Cup holders) and Isidro Diaz and Roberto Martinez from F.C. Balaguer.

The new arrivals are not just very good footballers but also very good friends. The ambitious transfer deal was set up through the Spanish arm of Latics owner Dave Whelan's sport chain, JJB. Had the club succeeded in tempting just one of the hot prospects to the lowly depths of the Endsleigh League it would have been surprising enough. All credit to Wigan for capturing the imagination of the public.

Transfer

The transfer of players has always been a feature of football and undoubtedly Latics' first major involvement in a transfer was when inside-right *Stan Bentham* moved from the Latics to Everton just before the 1934–35 season got underway at a record fee for a Cheshire League club.

During the 1947–48 season, full-back Johnny Ball was sold to Manchester United for £2,000. He was later to captain Bolton Wanderers. He returned to manage the Latics from December 1960 until resigning on 11 September 1963.

In 1957–58, Latics' left-half John Bramwell was sold to Everton for just over £3,000—it was a transfer fee that was to stand as a record for Wigan for several seasons. Bramwell was an Ashton-born player who really 'made good'. The powerfully built, tall Bramwell soon became a great favourite with the Springfield Park fans. It was obvious from the outset that Latics would have difficulty hanging on to Bramwell and just twelve short months after signing for Wigan, he joined Everton.

Peter Atherton.

In February 1980, Joe Hinnigan who was signed for a four-figure fee from South Liverpool, was transferred to Sunderland for a then record fee of £135,000.

Record Fees

When Peter Atherton left the club for Coventry City in August 1991, the Latics received £350,000. The largest amount paid by the club was in the summer of 1995 when we parted with £87,500 to acquire the services of Chris Lightfoot from Chester City.

Undefeated

The Latics have remained undefeated at home throughout three seasons and they are 1933–34 (Cheshire League, when we won all 21 games!), 1965–66 (Lancashire Combination) and 1969–70 (Cheshire League).

Our best and longest undefeated home sequence in the Football League is of 25 matches between 8 April 1985 and 16 March 1986.

The club's longest run of undefeated Football League matches, home and away, is 21 between 24 October 1981 and 12 March 1982, though in their Lancashire Combination days they had many a long unbeaten run. The longest of these ended on 5 November 1966, when Buxton had all the fireworks, putting an end to a run of 52 unbeaten league games going back to 15 September 1965, just not quite doubling the previous season's unbeaten record run.

Utility Players

A utility player is one of those particularly gifted footballers who can play in several, or even many different positions.

Harry Lyon was Wigan Athletic's answer to 'Roy of the Rovers'. He was arguably one of the greatest players ever to don the Latics' colours, and certainly the most popular. In 1964–65, he amassed the amazing total of 66 goals, whilst the following season he scored 61 goals. Against Doncaster Rovers at Belle Vue, he was forced to drop back and play full-back after Stuart Houghton had gone off injured, whilst in the replay at Springfield Park, he scored a magnificent hat-trick.

Later that season, both Wigan's 1st and 2nd team goalkeepers were injured. It was then that Harry Lyon stepped into the breach and went between the posts to play a blinder, as Latics won both the Cheshire League Cup Final (Altrincham a 2–0, h 3–1) and the Lancashire Junior Cup (Netherfield 2–0). In fact, in both of these games, Harry only

Mark Hilditch.

conceded one goal and that a Jackie Swindells penalty—his 83rd goal of the season!

After about the mid-1960s, players were encouraged to become more adaptable and to see their roles as less stereotyped. At the same time however, much less attention came to be paid to the implication of wearing a certain numbered shirt and accordingly, some of the more versatile players came to wear almost all the different numbered shirts at some stage or another, although this did not necessarily indicate a vast variety of positions.

Alex Cribley was certainly talented enough in midfield or defence to wear all but the No.10 shirt, whilst John Butler and Mark Hilditch wore nine of them in their careers with the Latics. In fact, John Butler had a spell in goal in the 1987–88 home match against Brighton when Nigel Adkins went off injured. Butler missed both Latics' Wembley appearances (Freight Rover and Mercantile) through injury, but did pick up a Wembley winners medal with Stoke City in the 1991–92 Autoglass competition.

Victories

In a Season

The Latics' greatest number of victories in a season is 33 from the 46 games of 1974–75 (Northern Premier League) whilst our most home victories (21) was achieved in 1933–34 (Cheshire League).

In a Match

Latics' best victories in their various league and cup competitions are as follows:

Home		
Cheshire League	12–1 *v.* Congleton Town	1937–38
Cheshire League Cup	7–0 *v.* Frickley Colliery (Rd 2)	1964–65
Lancashire Combination	9–0 *v.* Blackpool 'B'	1952–53
	9–0 *v.* Prescot Cables	1953–54
Lancashire Combination Cup	12–0 *v.* Stubshaw Cross (Rd 2)	1954–55
Lancashire Junior Cup	10–1 *v.* Earlestown (Rd 2)	1953–54
Lancashire Challenge Trophy	11–1 *v.* Darwen (Rd 2)	1969–70
Liverpool Non-League Cup	6–0 *v.* St Helens Town (Rd 1)	1954–55
Northern Premier League	7–0 *v.* Goole Town	1970–71
	7–0 *v.* Matlock	1973–74
	7–0 *v.* Great Harwood	1973–74
Football League	5–0 *v.* Peterborough United (Div. 4)	1981–82
	5–0 *v.* Swansea City (Div. 3)	1985–86
F.A. Cup	8–1 *v.* Fleetwood (2nd Q.Rd)	1962–63

Home

F.L. Cup	5–0 *v.* Wrexham (Rd 1 2nd Leg)	1989–90
Leyland DAF etc	6–0 *v.* Rochdale (Prelim Rd)	1985–86

Away

Cheshire League	6–1 *v.* Stafford Rangers	1965–66
Cheshire League Cup	3–0 *v.* Winsford United (semi-final)	1964–65
Lancashire Combination	7–1 *v.* Chorley	1950–51
Lancashire Combination Cup	6–1 *v.* Marine (Rd 2 Replay)	1959–60
Lancashire Junior Cup	7–0 *v.* Darwen (Rd 2)	1964–65
Lancashire Challenge Trophy	4–0 *v.* Horwich R.M.I. (Rd 1)	1975–76
Liverpool Non-League Cup	4–0 *v.* Burscough (semi-final)	1961–62
Northern Premier League	6–1 *v.* Lancaster City	1977–78
Football League	7–2 *v.* Scunthorpe United (Div 4)	1981–82
F.A. Cup	6–1 *v.* Carlisle United (Rd 1)	1934–35
F.L. Cup	3–0 *v.* Wrexham (Rd 1 1st Leg)	1984–85
Leyland DAF etc	3–1 *v.* Lincoln City (North semi-final)	1984–85

Wartime Football

As is well known, the whole sporting scene throughout the country was disrupted for six years, but there were games played and numerous 'leagues' were set up.

Athletic at the time asked to be kept informed by the authorities regarding the setting up of these leagues but the first real 'wartime'

soccer game at Springfield Park took place on 23 September 1939 between Latics and those arch rivals Chorley. Wigan were then members of the Cheshire League and Chorley the Lancashire Combination. The result was an astounding 8–2 victory for Wigan and although there were not many there to see it—money taken was just seventeen pounds three shillings and eleven pence—it turned out to be a thoroughly enjoyable match.

Latics over-ran their opponents in the first half, scoring six goals without reply, but the second half was a little more even, both sides scoring twice.

The team comprised mostly of local youngsters—such as Rainford and Rimmer from Prescot Cables and Cole, a very promising inside-forward who seemed to have enormous prospects. Unfortunately he had an early call-up and was killed at Dunkirk. The team was captained by a very experienced centre-half by the name of Hanna—a big Irishman who had seen service with Blackpool.

After the first wartime season, the club decided to close temporarily for the duration.

The ground was kept in reasonably good order by the older directors who were not called into the forces and they shared the expenses required from their own pockets. However, an old wooden stand which was the length of the pitch needed major repairs and the popular side shelter needed completely re-roofing.

When war in Europe ended in 1945, this repair work had to be completed—mostly by local volunteers—before the Cheshire League re-started in August 1945.

Weather

During the Latics' first season in the Football League, the match against Huddersfield Town at Springfield Park was the only English game played north of Leicester. The League's new boys turned out to be the area's lone football flag-bearers on what was another ice-age weekend. The club simply had the will to find a way to play and made the effort.

Conditions were by no means perfect, but 7,420 fans had a match to go to instead of listening to excuses from the 'big boys' content to have their games postponed.

Wigan boss Ian McNeill's recipe for beating the freeze was simple—about £150 of straw, plastic sheeting, some hot air on the worst ice-hit sections of Springfield Park and voluntary sweat and toil from a willing band of supporters.

Despite the slippery surface, Wigan played some superbly controlled football at times—the exact opposite to Huddersfield's basic boot-and-chase routine.

Two goals from skipper Noel Ward saw Latics win 2–1—the second a superb volley with just five minutes left.

Wigan Borough

Founded in 1921, they became that season one of the founder members of the Football League Third Division (North). Their first match saw them travel to Nelson who scored within seconds of the kick-off. Undaunted, the Boro' came back to win 2–1 with goals from Hodges and Twiss.

The club's early history was marked with relative success. In 1922–23 they recorded their record win of 9–1 over Lincoln and looked to be heading for promotion to Division Two, but slumped towards the end of the season and finished fifth.

The club's best seasons were recorded in 1928–29 when they reached the Third Round of the F.A. Cup only to lose 3–1 to the legendary Sheffield Wednesday side and finished fourth in the League, whilst the following season they beat Manchester City in the Manchester Senior Cup Final.

Throughout its ten-year history, the Boro' like its predecessors, suffered financial difficulties. In fact, it was only through the hard work of the supporters' club in raising enough money to pay the annual debts that the club survived for as long as it did.

The club acquired some fine players during their history, notably Frank Barson, the former Newcastle United and England centre-half, yet despite this, the club always had difficulty in raising the transfer

fees and in fact, towards the end of the 1930–31 season the financial situation became so critical that difficulty was experienced even in raising the players' wages.

The Football League, finding that the sum of £806 was owed to players in lieu of wages, issued an ultimatum; either pay up the arrears by 1 May or face the embarrassment of League suspension.

To avoid the acute embarrassment of League suspension, the club had sold its star players, but even these transfers failed to pull the club away from ruin, although additional sums of money were raised through the early selling of season tickets.

These tactics only proved to be delaying ones, for in 1931, Wigan Borough found itself as hard hit as everyone else in the year of the Great Depression. They were deep in trouble, but had at least survived to start the 1931–32 campaign. They started disastrously, losing 4–0 at Chester and to add insult to injury, it was Chester's first ever league game. There followed a 3–1 win over Hull City, but then a run of six consecutive defeats, with attendances rarely rising above the 3,000 mark.

The Football League again issued an ultimatum, but this time it was not suspension, but 'pay up or resign'. A public appeal was decided upon, but brought an appalling response and from there the decision to resign was taken.

Boro's last League game was played on 24 October 1931 against Wrexham at the Racecourse Ground—the result, a 5–0 win for the home side. The team did make one more appearance before going into voluntary liquidation in a last desperate attempt to fulfil their reserve team commitments. They won 2–1 at Southport then folded.

The Boro's epitaph was written by Frank Platt: 'From information I have gleaned from the books of the club, I have no hesitation in saying that the Association Football public of Wigan have shown once again, that they have no desire to maintain League Football in Wigan.'

Wigan County

Wigan County were formed in 1897 and were the first Association Football team to play at Springfield Park, when they entertained Burton Swifts in a friendly match on 1 September 1897.

They were the first but not the last club to suffer the fate of liquidation and extinction.

In the three years of their life, they were still fairly successful, and fielded an above average side in the Lancashire League. Perhaps their greatest moment of glory came at Ardwick in an F.A. Cup round when they outplayed Manchester City before eventually losing 1–0 thanks to a goalkeeping error.

 Cutting the first sod at the new Athletic ground (Springfield Park) 20 January 1897.

Wigan Town

Formed in season 1905–06, Wigan Town were the third attempt to establish football in Wigan. Yet like its predecessors it failed to outlive the magical three years hurdle and it was another thirteen years or so before anyone tried again.

Wigan United

Formed in 1901, they competed for two seasons in the Lancashire Combination before folding in 1904. In season 1901–02 they shared Springfield Park with Wigan Rugby League Football Club, using the ground on alternate Saturdays.

Wigan United also have the distinction of being drawn away to Stalybridge in the Third Round of the Rawcliffe Cup. As the ground was waterlogged they declined to play, but the referee decided against them and allowed the home team to kick-off and dribble the ball down the field and place it into the net!

Youth Cup

One of former manager Brian Tiler's first jobs after taking over from Les Rigby was to ensure that the young side Rigby had built up did not disintegrate.

On the contrary, the side went from strength to strength, winning the Lancashire Youth Cup and having a tremendous run in the F.A. Youth Cup competition.

Latics were taking a lesson from their seniors and provided a few shocks in knocking out higher grade teams in the Youth Cup, before they themselves were put out of the 1973–74 competition by First Division Wolves at Molyneux after a draw at Springfield Park.

The first clash took place on 8 December 1973 in front of a large Springfield Park crowd. Despite some fierce Latics pressure, the match ended in a goalless draw with a Wigan player missing an absolute sitter in the final minute!

The second match at Molyneux was totally different; a fast open game ended with Latics going down 3–2, but in defeat, the local boys earned glowing praise from the officials of the Wolves club.

Also in a youth team game, Latics' youngest player to represent the club in the Football League, Stephen Nugent, once scored 9 goals!

Zambia

In October 1978, Zambia became the first national team to play at Springfield Park. Coached by Brian Tiler, who managed our Northern Premier League Championship side of 1975, Zambia had emerged as one of Africa's top soccer nations.

They had been eliminated from the World Cup finals that year in a three-way play-off; international victories included wins against Algeria, Kenya, Morocco, Nigeria and Zaire, but they couldn't beat the Latics who won 2–1.

ATHLETIC
WIGAN

OFFICIAL PROGRAMME — 15p

TOUR MATCH

v.

National Team of Zambia

Wednesday, 11th October, 1978 — Kick-off 7-30 p.m.

The programme for the visit of the Zambian National Team coached by former Latics boss Brian Tiler.